# Waking Up Together

*Other books by Paul Williams:*

Outlaw Blues
Pushing Upward
Time Between
Das Energi
Apple Bay
Right to Pass
Coming
Heart of Gold
Dylan—What Happened?
The Book of Houses (with Robert Cole)
The International Bill of Human Rights (editor)
Common Sense

# Waking Up Together

## Paul Williams

## illustrated by Darrin Brenner

ENTWHISTLE BOOKS
Glen Ellen

*Waking Up Together* cover logo designed by Neal Lekwa.
Back cover photograph by Donna N. Ansell.

ISBN 0-934558-13-2

First printing, May 1984.

File under:  Philosophy.

Printed in the U.S.A.

This first printing of 2000 copies is a preview edition, not
offered for sale in bookstores nor made available to review
media.
Additional copies may be obtained by sending $12.50 per
copy plus $1 postage to the address below; see order form at
the back of this book.

You may write to Paul Williams or Darrin Brenner in care of
Entwhistle Books.

Published by:     Entwhistle Books
                  Box 611
                  Glen Ellen, CA 95442

*For Judith,*
*who opened the door,*
*and Donna,*
*who walked in.*

# CONTENTS

# A Note to the Reader

This book is organized so that there is an entry for every day of the year: twelve chapters, one for each month, and 29, 30, or 31 little sections in each chapter. The purpose of this is simply to make the book more fun: you can read it straight through, you can open it anywhere and see what you get, or you can look up today's date or your birthday or someone else's birthday.

I haven't labored to make any connection between the dates of the entries and what I've written for those dates. If you do find any connections, please give credit to the Gods of coincidence and chance, and not to me.

In particular I want to explain that I did not write these entries on the dates given. This is not a diary in any ordinary sense. I began writing in February and finished in November, and often didn't write for a week and then wrote five or more sections in a single night. So if you wonder why I have blood on my face in the section called "April 7," it might help to know that "April 5" could have been (and was) written the same evening.

There are a number of books that have used this almanac format; my inspiration was a book by Will Cuppy that I owned and loved as a child, called *How to Get from January to December*. I'd like to thank Mr. Cuppy for giving me the idea, and I hope this present book may also be useful in helping a few of us get through the year and back to the moment.

# Chapter One

# JANUARY

**JANUARY 1**

I claim to want to write about some or all of the thousand things that run through my attention. And yes I know people are interested in many of these and I know I have much to say that is worthwhile and I have the ability to say it well, to make it fresh, make it breathe. People tell me, "you've written so much"—my own experience is an almost suffocating silence. I write so seldom. I've written so little these last many years, and I have so much more to give.

And then it all gets bottlenecked, when the word gets

out that I'm heading for the typewriter, not for business but to really Say Something, all those new and ancient energies rush for their chance to be said, be shared, and they crash into each other and fight for priority and what seems to happen is that nothing happens, it's kind of sad.

So here I am. Shall I talk about my experience this afternoon of hearing Bob Dylan on tape read his poem "Last Thoughts on Woody Guthrie"? Or should I save that for an essay or book only about Dylan, to be read by only his fans? Shall I say something about my vision of humankind in this 1980s? Well yes, I'd like to. But what's my context? Who'm I speaking to? Are you there?

What's my image of myself? What's getting in the way of just letting it flow? How do I make better use of what I have, allow myself to be more of who I am? Maybe I just have to make a choice. Like I could choose to go on writing this however it comes out. Okay, I so choose.


### JANUARY 2

*Waking Up Together*

. . . waking up together suggests having gone to sleep together, and that suggests lovemaking, sexual intimacy. If my subject tonight is in fact human awakening, species or trans-species awakening, imminent or currently taking place, may we then imagine that sexual play, perhaps orgasm, followed by sleep and even dreams together, has in some sense already taken place? And now we are stretching to greet the dawn, and how do we feel about this? How do you feel? May I ask?


### JANUARY 3

Today I wanted to give someone a hundred dollars (a particular person, to make it easier for her to take a plane and come and visit me). I decided that I would do it in any event, and that what would make it really easy would be for

2

someone to give me a hundred dollars today. So I put that thought out, and let go of it. And later, without my asking or saying anything, a friend while we were talking suddenly pulled out his wallet and counted out some bills and handed them to me. I thanked him and stuffed them in my pocket and later found out that he had given me (of course) exactly $100. He didn't know about my thought. And yet he knew.

## JANUARY 4

### In the Midnight Hour

"I'm gonna wait till the midnight hour, that's when my love comes tumbling down . . ." —Wilson Pickett. And I've been planning for years to write a book about the midnight hour, which to me is a certain place beyond or outside of time that I have visited again and again, in a special moment with a friend, on a sexual adventure, at a party particularly a party that lasts for days, like a convention or other gathering, sometimes listening to music or all alone and for no reason at all, boom, I'm in that timeless place, and I love it. All of your past and future are with you in the midnight hour. It's like a bar full of old friends and new friends, everyone you've known or will know throughout your life. And many new things can happen. And it feels so familiar, like home, I belong here and am free to be everything I am. "I'm gonna hold you in my arms in the midnight hour."

## JANUARY 5

A lot depends on what we imagine is possible. Thinking it possible may or may not create it, but thinking it impossible certainly defines your limits.

When we cry with joy, "I can't believe it!", another part is saying, "I refuse to believe it." Watch out.

3

This is fun. I know what I'm doing. I'm pretending that it might be all right to be who I really am.

I want your love and attention so much, I shut up for fear I won't get it.

And then I don't get it.

So how come I'm willing to come out of my hiding hole all of a sudden? Could it possibly have anything to do with the great loss of security (marriage, identity) I so recently suffered/created? Could it be some stupid stubborn part of me is finally temporarily convinced I have nothing to lose?

This is fun. I have a thousand voices, and they're all one voice. I think I was ashamed of that for a long time. I wonder why?

Oh, I know why writing takes so much energy. It's because of the decisions. Each line, each word can be a decision. If it's no fun, it's utterly exhausting. And on the other side, if each decision is made with love, imagine how much consciousness can be expressed! You could lay an entire planet bare this way.

Einstein came into this century with the right attitude. If you want to and believe it possible, there's no secret that can't be told. This whole situation here's an open book, if we care to read it. God's not holding anything back.

No secret that can't be told. If you want to be loved, give yourself away.


## JANUARY 7

Waking up together to me implies recognition: that we not merely wake up simultaneously, but in fact recognize each other, recognize that we are here and going through this together. I see my awakening in you sometimes more than I see it in myself.

As I awaken, as I open my eyes seemingly for the first time, I see you and you have the same beautiful childlike Godstruck look on your face that I imagine I have: big silly grin, look at this amazing universe I've been reborn into. And gratitude.

What would it take for you to recognize how conscious, and how powerful, you as an individual are becoming?

We are coming into our own conscious power. That's frightening, I know—at least, it can be. But could it really be more frightening than the unconscious power (personal anger, nuclear weapons) we've already aimed at ourselves?

My vision of humankind in this 1980s is that we are coming into our conscious power: awareness of each person's ability to shape a loving universe starting now, and willingness to allow ourselves to drink more openly from the fountain of God's love.

All we have to do to save ourselves from annihilation is be willing to use our power.


## JANUARY 8

A holistic doctor, looking at a sick patient, sees an inherently healthy person with a transient condition that requires immediate attention. The doctor's response is determined less by the nature of the illness than by the nature of that person's health, the total picture of that person's natural energy flow. Support the flow, so that it may better do its job of correcting the imbalance. (Never attack the imbalance directly and in a hostile fashion; that only strengthens it, feeds its resistance.)

Now let's apply this to our desire to heal the world.

First, let us notice that the world we live in is essentially, intrinsically healthy. And let us acknowledge at the same time that there is evidence of illness, of imbalance, and that it is debilitating and in fact life-threatening. Immediate attention is required.

(Lack of attention may lead to famine, genocide, ecological catastrophe, nuclear holocaust.)

How shall we proceed, once we have decided not to deny that the problem exists?

The most important action we can take is to notice, support, encourage the natural flow of healing energy from person to person in our immediate environment and all over the planet.

That may not sound like much, but it's the shortest possible path to the results we want. And it works.


### JANUARY 9

People are learning to channel healing energy with their hands. I see many people who have been drawn into studying bodywork, massage, without really knowing why. It is an immediate, physical, spiritual way of being of service. We want to keep in touch with each other. Somehow we know that's important.


### JANUARY 10

This is a time of opportunity. We are like children who say, "there's nothing to do!", when in fact there are thousands of things that need doing, among them many that are great fun and highly worthwhile and made to order for a person with your skills and personality and experience. And still you hang out in uncertainty. That's fine, as long as you are honest and admit to yourself that it isn't that there's nothing to do, or too much to do—the precise problem is that there *is* something to do, and it means so much to you that you're afraid your whole universe will become dislocated if you allow yourself to get involved in this.

You're right.

How much longer can you go on pretending there's nothing to do and anyway you don't have anything to offer?

Maybe you're waiting for the fear to go away. But it won't. The secret is, let the fear be there and go ahead and do what you have to do anyway.


### JANUARY 11

I seem to be contradicting myself. In my book *Das Energi* I wrote that fear must be eliminated from the mind the instant it is recognized. "Accept that fear is not needed,

6

that there is *never* a reason to let it live." And now I hear myself saying, "let the fear be there."

Maybe I changed my mind.

But that suggests that I want to take back or change the words I wrote earlier. And I could, I suppose. I could admit that I was wrong and apologize and explain my new point of view.

That would be fine. But I can't do it. Those words in *Das Energi* have helped a lot of people, many people have let me know that they created great results for themselves at a difficult moment in their lives and that my comments on fear seemed to play a part in that. I know there is great power in the truth that some folks find in those words; for me to renounce them now might not change anything (since I don't control the words; they're out in the universe and can't be recalled) but it would certainly be dishonest.

So what's the deal, Paul? Is there or is there not ever a reason to let fear live?

Hmm. I think I'm ready to look at this now.

### JANUARY 12

There is never any benefit to be gained from indulging in fear. Fear attacks the mind, it takes over, it starts calling the tune, after a while it looks like your friend, your protector. It tells you what to say and do so nothing scary will happen. If you don't obey, it scares you to prove its point. Fear is a tyrant. It keeps us from getting what we really want and being who we really are. Fear is the enemy of awareness. It imitates awareness—it mugs awareness and throws it in a closet and puts on its uniform and then tinkers with all the information coming in, so that we think we're perceiving reality and in fact we only know what fear wants us to know. And if we get suspicious and try to investigate, fear does the investigation for us and gives itself a clean bill of health.

*Das Energi* tells us not to try to use reason to protect ourselves from fear. That is correct. Reason means thinking, and it happens that fear is fed by thinking the way a flame is fed by oxygen. Remove the oxygen and the fire goes out. Stop thinking, stop reasoning, and fear will at least stop growing. If you are rigorous in not thinking about it, it will probably disappear.

This requires discipline. It won't work to think about whether or not it's time to stop thinking. ("Thinking" in this context means "thinking about"—it doesn't mean stop being conscious. It means stop the chatter, the internal dialogue, stop whatever your mind is doing and just allow yourself to be here.) So we train our minds to notice the first signs of fear and to respond by shutting down the thought process (not the awareness) in order to deprive the fear of its fuel.

*Das Energi* says of fear, "stamp it out!" That's appropriate insofar as it conjures up the quickness and earnestness of the response. I was trying to help people teach themselves a reflex or automatic response, and I continue to believe that such a reflex (fear: stamp it out) can be essential to survival.

If you don't have that reflex, if you experience yourself feeling helpless in the face of each new onslaught of fear that comes along, you might want to read pp. 39–44 of that book.

However: I do want to note that "stamp it out" is a rather violent image (the same passage also says, "shoot first, ask questions later"). It serves its purpose, but it leaves something out. I wanted to emphasize the quickness of the response, but the words I chose also emphasize forcefulness. And that can be misleading.

Stamping on a fire puts it out by depriving it of oxygen. Throwing a blanket over it is less forceful but has the same effect. Water also puts out fire by depriving it of oxygen. As a volunteer fireman, I know there's a natural tendency to want to hit a fire with as hard a stream of water as possible— and often that just pushes the fire around, spreads it. We're taught that in most situations you do much better with a gentle, diffuse stream of water, called "a fog."

Where am I going with this? *Das Energi* says, "Fear is a disease. It blocks the flow of energy. It spreads. It destroys. If it is not stopped, it kills."

Many people tell me they feel that parts of my writing are channelled. That's a term that can easily create misunderstanding—my experience is that yes, it is channelled, but the source is not some departed spirit or ethereal being; the source, dear reader, is you. Be that as it may, let's just say that

8

what I'm doing right now is trying to resolve an apparent contradiction in this channelled material. For the sake of argument and intellectual exercise we'll assume that these transmissions are all true; that means we have to take a closer look at the places where they "seem" to contradict each other.


## JANUARY 13

"Fear is a disease." And in section 8 of this present work I speak of illness as an imbalance in a person's energy flow, and say, "Never attack the imbalance directly and in a hostile fashion; that only strengthens it, feeds its resistance."

Elementary rules of logic and grammar suggest that these two sentences can be combined into one that reads: "Never attack fear directly and in a hostile fashion; that only strengthens it, feeds its resistance."

Sounds true to me. "Stamp it out," indeed!


## JANUARY 14

My God, the rain keeps pouring down. A year ago January the rains filled all the hundred-year flood plains, and now they say this year, this storm, is worse. I don't feel immediately threatened: my house is neither on a hill nor too near the creek (let alone ocean; homes by the ocean are taking a terrific pounding this week, up and down the California coast). I just feel in the middle of life, as usual. There's so much of it!

All right, so how am I going to resolve this paradox about fear? On the one hand the way to handle it is to accept that there's never a reason to let it live, to stamp it out automatically the moment it appears; on the other hand the secret of not being controlled by fear is to stop waiting for it to go away, to just allow it to be there and not let it prevent you from doing what you want to do.

So we could take the attitude that there's a direct opposition here: "stamp it out" versus "let it be." And we could push me around and try to get me to say which one I really believe in. We could take sides and be in favor of one approach or the other and root for our favorite. And you know we often think this way: when two points of view seem to contradict each other, we try to find out which is right and which is wrong.

Or we could take an alternate attitude: there's no opposition here. Two of the many techniques for handling fear have been presented, or at least alluded to; which of the many (if any) you use depends on what makes sense to you, what speaks to your situation, at a given moment.

### JANUARY 15

In fact, the two approaches have many similarities. They are both simple, practical techniques for not letting fear be the cause of what happens in your life. In one case fear is rejected, in the other it is ignored; in both cases it is kept at a distance. These are techniques for detachment. It could be said that in either case what you're doing is refusing to play fear's game.

What I've noticed is that a lot of us (probably all of us, at one time or another) are busy trying to stamp out fear or get rid of it in some way. This doesn't work—stamping out fear works fine, but *trying to* stamp it out or *trying to* overcome it is something else again. "Trying to" means putting energy in without actually doing it. So "trying to" do something about fear means putting your attention and energy on fear, means not doing what you want to do because you're convinced that fear has to be dealt with first. Means putting fear first. Means being ruled by fear, however subtly.

Now what a lot of us do when we hear that we're hung up in "trying to," is, we try harder! "Got to stop 'trying to' stamp out fear and start actually stamping it out, so that means I'm not doing it, got to try even harder." Whew. To get out of trying, we try even more. Sounds crazy, but I know I do it and I'll bet you do too. We "try" to stop "trying." Doesn't work!

10

What's the alternative? How do we get out of this trap of trying?

Surrender. Let the fear be there.

## JANUARY 16

An example I like to use is this: most of us are very afraid of speaking or performing in front of an audience. And many of us would actually like to speak or perform, if only we could overcome that fear. We look at people who do go up in front of audiences, and we think, "That person's not afraid. That's why he (she) can do it."

Wrong. This is an idea we use to separate ourselves from what we want to do. ("I couldn't do that.") The truth is that every performer, every public speaker, feels fear every time he or she walks out to face an audience. (If they don't, they've numbed themselves in some way and probably won't give a good performance.) They all feel fear.

They feel fear and they go ahead and do it anyway. They let the fear be there, and they walk out and they look at the audience and they start speaking, or dancing, or singing.

Can they do this because they feel *less* fear than you or I would? No, not necessarily. They can do it because they're willing to pay the price, willing to go out even though fear is there, willing to believe (even when they don't really believe it) that they're bigger than the fear and can't be pushed around by it. They choose not to be ruled by fear. That may look like pushing it away, or it may look like letting it be there. You can even do both at once.

You can do both at once because stamping it out is something you do when the fear *encroaches,* advances beyond its limits, makes the slightest move to start taking your attention, your space. "Letting it be there" is a good way of not giving it attention. It's like a brush fire that's been contained. The fire crews surround it, let it burn itself out—and jump on it immediately any time it starts to cross the fire line. So they use the "stamp it out" reflex and they let the fire be there, both at once.

11

Another image I have that I find useful is "breathing out fear." Feel yourself breathing in courage (or love, or clarity) on the in-breath, and just release some of your fear as you breathe out. Let it ride out on your out-breath. The key to this is not to imagine you're going to get rid of all of it. You're just releasing the overflow, breathing out the excess. The fear will still be there—but because you're breathing out the excess, it isn't a problem.

One more thing about words: notice that in talking about "letting the fear be there" I have never once said that we let it be there because it's needed. From my point of view, I haven't actually contradicted the statement that "there is never a reason to let fear live." Or perhaps I need to re-phrase that: there's never a reason to let it encroach. But the underlying intent of the words stays the same: don't let fear try to justify itself, don't listen to its reasons. Letting it be there, stamping it out, breathing it out are all effective ways of not listening to its reasons. Denying fear ("I never feel fear any more") or trying to overcome it are not effective techniques.

All this chatter of mine is not really about ideas. It's about giving the reader a chance to discover what works for you.


### JANUARY 17


My dear friend who died one year ago today wrote a book—the last of his fifty books—called *The Transmigration of Timothy Archer.* By Philip K. Dick. This book is so rich that although I read it once in manuscript, I now find I can never read more than a few pages at a time, it overwhelms me. It's wonderful. It happens to be full of pain, but only in the precise sense that pain is awareness: "your love cuts like a knife." Pages so full of awareness it's as if Phil still lives, and of course he does. "I dreamed I saw Joe Hill last night, Alive as you or me. Said I, but Joe, you're ten years dead; I never died, says he."

Hello, Phil, wherever you are. I can feel you here with me. I love you.

## January 18

I saw a double rainbow yesterday. Last weekend a tornado passed within 100 yards of the house where my younger son was staying. No one was hurt. Two people were killed in the rain on Friday when a five-ton truck veered into their car. I was there; I helped perform CPR on the man and later rode with him in the ambulance, holding an oxygen mask to his face. He was pronounced dead at the hospital. His wife was pronounced dead at the accident scene. I read that in the newspaper and realized that I had been one of the ones pronouncing her dead. Today I bought a week's worth of groceries for myself and the two boys, and made corn fritters for dinner.

## January 19

*Men and Women*

People have been encouraging me to write a book about men and women. I admit the subject interests me, but I have some difficulty imagining what the book would look like, what shape it would take. Maybe that's good—whenever I do have an idea of what something will look like it always turns out different anyway.

I was in love last fall with a Swiss-German woman named Judith, and one of the plans we cooked up during our brief, intense time together was that we would collaborate on a book about men and women. So when people would ask me whether I was working on something, I'd mention that. And now that Judith and I have experienced some of the difficulties that befall men and women, now that my sanity depends on knowing that I have no way of knowing whether I'll ever see her again, let alone write a book with her (well actually I could write a book with her without seeing her, couldn't I?), and now that I actually am writing a book which is designed to be about everything and anything I feel like talking about, well, I guess if I do write a book about men and women in the near future sometime, this is likely to be it.

I wonder what it will look like?

I was sitting with Judith and another bright 23-year-old

13

beauty named Esther, at a dining table in the guesthouse in the Swiss Alps where we were doing a workshop, there was a lot going on between the three of us (and Judith had to translate it all, since Esther knew very little English and I was helpless in Swiss-German), and anyway I suddenly had one of those revelations that change your point of view forever but sound idiotic when you try to explain them. What I realized was that my relationships just are what they are. A great weight fell away from me. All three of us were laughing.

### JANUARY 20

A friend was over the other day talking about this lady-friend he's been very close with for years and now they're starting to look seriously at the possibility of being lovers, and he wants very much to make love with her and have this friendship become a sexual relationship, and he's also very scared that this could spoil everything, could mess up this active friendship that's so important to both of them. And he has every reason to be scared, and so does she. Experience tells us that when friends become lovers, sometimes it works and sometimes it doesn't, and when it doesn't it's very difficult for the friendship to be what it was. So the risk is quite real.

Speaking for myself, I love courtship but I hate rejection. Yet without the possibility of rejection, courtship would be meaningless. How can you win what you already have? And also, without the possibility of success, without a goal, courtship would be meaningless. That's one aspect of the sexual act we seldom consider: that without the consummation it implies, and the difficulties that surround it, we could never enjoy the pleasures of courtship. Putting everything else aside, we just have to make sex something special and hard to attain, in order to have all the pleasures associated with trying to get someone to go there with you or with having someone try to get you to go there with them.

There's a lot of pain associated with these things, too. So we all have mixed feelings about sex.

Just notice, if you will, that for better or worse, sex is what makes romance possible.

14

Now, in the case mentioned above, this guy and this gal are friends, they share a lot, they enjoy each other's company. And what's true (based on what's happening now) is that they've been engaged in a very long, drawn-out courtship. It's been a lot of fun, and now it's coming to an end, and naturally they have mixed feelings about that. If it's going to be replaced by something even better, well that's great, but if it's going to destroy itself in chasing after the false hope of something better, well, what a shame.

But notice that there's this feeling that reaching for sexual love threatens friendship. It's true. But let us also notice, if my premise that this has been one long courtship is correct, that reaching for sexual love is what created friendship in the first place, and, believe it or not, what sustained it all this time.

Something that's true about sex is that even between friends, even between lovers, it presents tremendous possibilities for rejection. And the reason that friendship has trouble sometimes surviving the sexual act is that friendship naturally has trouble surviving rejection. ("What do you mean, you love me, but I'm not your type?!") The only times that friendship seems to easily survive a sexual experiment that doesn't become great mutual sexual love is when it turns out that sex with the other was equally unspecial for both people. In which case, things might be okay, provided no one has lost their sense of humor.

What do we want? Well, we know what we think we want, and what we think we don't want. And when we experience wanting someone, we assume it's because that person can give us what we think we want (why else would I feel this way?). And when they do give us what we thought we wanted, we sometimes feel like it's not what we want after all. I guess I don't know what I want. Such an empty feeling. And then someone else walks by, and we experience that we definitely *want* them. Such a full feeling. Such a crazy, confusing mess. Such a gorgeous mystery.

### JANUARY 24

It's Monday morning. I feel I don't really have time to work on this book this morning, and I'm aware how silly that sounds as I say it. I'm a writer—so what could be more important than doing my writing? I'm also a single father, at the moment, and that often takes precedence; but that's not the consideration right now, I've already made breakfast and box lunches for the boys and they've gone to school, I baked bread last night, I have a plan for dinner tonight and everything's under control except the dishes in the sink.

So what's all this about time? Well, a neighbor is coming over in an hour and we're going to go out and have lunch together. He's not a pretty girl, so it wouldn't be that difficult for me to cancel, but it wouldn't be polite (since it's not truly necessary) and anyway my intuition tells me, have lunch with this guy, it's part of the plan. Like maybe some passing item in the conversation will have an important triggering effect allowing my mind to take the next step in some major item it's working out, whatever. No way of knowing. Maybe he and I will become great friends. Maybe I'll fall in love with the waitress.

It's not just the lunch date. Monday means mail to answer, and time to catch up on the mail I'd planned to send on Friday or Saturday. Particularly I'm eager to write my dear friend Jules about the terrific manuscript he sent me, two years in the making, the story of his death in and rebirth following a car wreck. One effect the book had on me already is I suddenly realized, though I've known Jules' car wreck story for years, that the extreme damage (I believe his jaw was well inside his partner's skull) and extraordinary recovery (both lived, and Jules defied all odds to do so) have strong

16

implications for me as a first responder at accident scenes. (Something I do because I'm a fireman, and we get called and are closer and thus arrive some minutes before the ambulance.) What I mean is, I think I'm going to try even harder, to cut people out of cars even when they look hopeless and see if there isn't some way to start CPR even as we're cutting and they're crunched in the vehicle (my instructor says just doing the breaths can help). After all, one of those people might be a miracle like Jules, and I sure am aware of how much it means to all of us to still have him around. (Or, as he tells us, to have around the new person who was born from the wreckage after "Julian"—his former self—died.)

Notice how the pressure of time has me writing fast? It's kind of an experiment, I mean I knew I didn't have much "time" and I decided to hit the typewriter anyway and see what these conditions might produce.

And I have on my conscience an application for non-profit status for a community organization that I've promised to take care of—I ain't an attorney but I can do it as good as most, better than many—got a phone call prodding me on this A.M., and I know it's time. And all I have to do is clear some space to give it some hours of undivided attention. Oh those hours of undivided attention! So modest a wish, so close at hand, and yet so hard to grasp.

And yet a pretty girl (attractive woman) can get hours of my undivided attention almost any time, hours I would have sworn didn't and couldn't exist in my schedule. It's almost as though she can (I can, with her inspiration) create time, out of nothing. What power. It's almost embarrassing.

And letters to answer, and other "stuff I have to do today." Funny how the stuff I have to do can so totally get in the way of what I really want to do. And I let it. Or else I don't. Lately, I don't, more and more. It's a liberation. I'm allowing myself to take a different point of view.

There. That's quite a satisfactory section of talk. And I still have half an hour before my friend comes over. Will I write a letter, or work on the incorporation? Nah. I think I'll read the paper. Make a phone call. Maybe wash the dishes.

17

## January 25

Long ago I learned that if one has a message to give the world, that message can be boiled down to "I exist." "I am." Bob Dylan's songs, Picasso's paintings, Einstein's equations, Gandhi's nonviolent actions, all are expressions of a single statement: I am. And it is a joyous statement. Even its hatred is filled with love.

## January 26

Now in the midnight hour I make some phone calls and soon the house is filled with guests. David comes by with the gal he used to date when we went to the Cape together in '63, and I get to be fifteen again. Alan brings some abalone that survived the recent storms, and we pound 'em and fry 'em. My wife shows up for an hour, very excited to tell of her adventures and successes on tour, and to share a couple of new songs—they're fabulous!—she wakes up the boys and gives them big hugs and lets them know everything's all right, and then back to Germany. Phil calls—"Paul? It's Phil"—and completely ignoring the fact that he's known to be dead, asks me if I have time to hear about something very important that just happened to him. I smile. My voice smiles. And Nancy is in my arms again like she was this afternoon in the car in the silence just after we saw *Gandhi* together. And I put on a tape of T-Bone Burnett and everybody starts dancing.

## January 27

You'd have to be crazy to read a sentence like this.

## January 28

Waking up (awakening) is sometimes a gradual process, sometimes a very sudden one. How shall we define "wake"? My first thought is, "to return to consciousness." Awakening

18

is like realization, but it is a gentler image to me, those eyes just keep on opening, wonders upon wonders. Good morning, good morning, good morning, as the Beatles once said. Spring of 1967 certainly felt like a time of awakening. So does the spring of '83.

Waking up together means becoming conscious together. Remembering who we are. And loving ourselves again.

## JANUARY 29

If I had time, if I had energy, I would tell you of a great many things. When I have time, when I have energy, I will tell you of a great many things. I have time and I have energy, and I am telling you and giving to you now.

## JANUARY 30

Thank you for sharing this with me. The truth about men and women is attraction/repulsion, many people would deny that much of the time, but their actions give them away. Attraction/repulsion looks something like this: we let ourselves be pulled, then we push ourselves away.

The first week of high school physics, the teacher asked us to invent some theories about what holds matter together, what is the glue of atoms and molecules. One boy suggested "love"—we all snickered but the teacher treated it seriously, like, who knows? And now I can't get it out of my mind that that kid was right, and in that moment of laughter in Doc's basement classroom we were as close as anyone's been to the essential mysteries of our time.

And that thought is followed by a strange vision of the Easter Be-In in Central Park in 1967, tens of thousands of us letting go of everything else and becoming pure energy particles. Right. I know what that feels like.

And as I experience love and the confusion of male/female attraction/repulsion and notice the strange rules we conduct our lives under (not the acquired rules but the innate ones, those are most fascinating), I have to admit I know exactly what it must feel like to be an atomic particle and exactly why (I can feel it, not explain it) they do what they do in relation to each other. It has to do with personal power, the desire to express it and the fear of letting it loose. I know now why the universe and I are so unstable, so restless, and why we love to go on creating order (it's beautiful!) as long as we don't actually ever have to arrive there. To arrive is to stop. We don't want to come yet.

### JANUARY 31

What is possible is a matter of choice. Let's get together and do something really wonderful.

# Chapter Two
# FEBRUARY

## FEBRUARY 1

Now I'm working on this book because I've started and I don't want to stop. No, that can't be the only reason, because I just put aside six pages I wrote in the last few days and I'm starting this chapter over again. That suggests that some part of me thinks it can tell the difference between what fits and what doesn't fit, what's "good" and what's not good enough. Some part of me is apparently willing to act like it's in touch with the real reasons I'm doing this work.

One reason for caution on my part is I notice that when I claim to know why I'm doing what I'm doing, I'm very often wrong. Looking back from a while later, I can usually see some things that were going on with me that I just wasn't aware of at the time. And you know, no matter how "smart," how aware, how conscious I think I've become, this still turns out to be true. Is it possible we're running in a race in which we can never quite catch up with ourselves?

When I started, "Waking Up Together" was just a working title, and I'm still not sure how I feel about it. But people have such a positive response to the title when I mention it, and it does seem in some way to connect with all aspects of the work that I'm aware of, that I suspect it's going to stick, I mean I'm stuck with it.

And people ask me, "What's the book about?", and I don't have an answer. (After 13 years I don't have an answer to what *Das Energi* is about, either.) I say, "awakening." Then I say, "Well, it's about anything and everything, whatever I feel like talking about." But I notice that's not true. There are a number of subject areas that interest me that I know I'm not going to include to any great degree in this book. They don't fit. Or anyway, my impulse to talk about them in a very specific way (like comparing two versions of an unreleased Bob Dylan song) doesn't fit. Which again suggests, in a back-handed way, that there *is* a focus to the manuscript, it isn't just a place to dump everything.

I don't really want to "know" what that focus is. What I want is to be able to share this with you, to tell the truth, to know I'm in touch with my inspiration, to be able to keep going. Just let me keep going. Hmm, that's where I began this section, isn't it?


### FEBRUARY 2

More and more I notice it's possible to do the right thing without understanding what's going on. And that it's possible to understand exactly what's happening and still do everything wrong.

### FEBRUARY 3

I personally believe that a great awakening is taking place on this planet, and also that it's made up of hundreds of millions of small awakenings, experienced by each of us, as simple as getting out of bed in the morning and as profound as watching the sun come up.

What can we do with this information? Well for one thing, we could relax, and wait and see what the new day will bring.

And if there are any choices we have to make, we could go ahead and make them now, and not put them off any longer.

The *I Ching* says, "If there is still somewhere one has to go, hastening brings good fortune. If there is no longer anywhere one has to go, return brings good fortune." And it goes on to remind us that what the world needs a lot of at this time is forgiveness.

### FEBRUARY 4

Forgive yourself, unconditionally. Don't condition your forgiveness on promises. Don't promise to do or not to do anything. Acknowledge who you really are, and how you are behaving, and love the person you are, especially where it's most difficult to do so.

If you can truly forgive yourself, with no conditions, no promises, and live naked every day, love and forgiveness for others will fall as naturally from you as tears.

### FEBRUARY 5

What could a woman possibly offer a man? Well, she could give him her attention, and truly be interested in who he is and the stories he has to tell. She could motivate him to be as beautiful and alive as he really is—and reward him with her smile.

She could create with him a space for play that is inexhaustible, so that his spirit might always dance, with hers, in an endless cycle of mutual inspiration. She could let him turn his instinct for love-making into a joyous and passionate expression of and surrender to God's love. She could hold him in her arms.

She could open him, and awaken his ability to be in the present, to "be there" for people. She could comfort him when he's afraid of his power, and support him in his courage that acknowledges the fear and still goes ahead and takes the risk. She can let him know that he can be loved even when he is naked.

She can give him a part of God that he can touch and love in every way; she can be his inspiration when he is not with his purpose and when he is with his purpose; she can give him a reason to do his very best.


## FEBRUARY 6

What could a man possibly offer a woman? Shelter from the storm, and a home in this world, a heart that's true that she can lean on and go out from and always come home to.

He can give her the support and protection she needs to allow herself to be as powerful and creative as she really is.

He can give her peace when she's in confusion, and stimulation when she's depressed. He can share her joy with her, and affirm that what she experiences is reality. He can let her know that she is loved for being exactly who she is, that she is loved even at her most naked, no mask.

He can give her security and freedom.


## FEBRUARY 7

I think you already know that there is no significance to the words "man" and "woman" in these little essays, that you can go back and change every "he" to "she" and "she" to "he" and whatever truth is in the words won't change. If there is a significance, it has to do with the fact that the writer sees himself as a man, and so the first of the two essays is about what he wants or what he has experienced receiving, and the second, shorter essay is about what he imagines he has to offer. And for him too, there is a lot to be learned in noticing that he can offer to a woman what he says a woman can offer a man.

### FEBRUARY 8

Perhaps in the midnight hour men and women sometimes exchange veils. We have to exchange them because if we take them off altogether we aren't men and women any more. And sometimes we do that too. Sometimes sex is the only thing that can take us beyond sexual attraction (and its effects and distractions). Sometimes renouncing sex is the only thing that can take us beyond sexual attraction (and its effects and distractions). Sometimes we get so caught up in just being together that we forget all those other things, and just hang out in being here, and that's when all our friends come around and tell us how much they love us too.

### FEBRUARY 9

I'm sleepy, I'm waiting for the pizza to be served on the Balboa Peninsula, Newport Beach, Orange County. My two boys are with me, and my friend Peggy who leads workshops with me. We did a one-day "empowerment" workshop yesterday, and tomorrow we drive back to northern California. I need a cup of tea. I won't settle for coffee.

I think of lots of things to say when I'm not writing, or even while I put down my pen between paragraphs (pen now, not typewriter, because I'm on the road). But when I start writing, something else comes out. The river already moved on. And my job is to be in the moment.

Now we're in Orange Julius. I got my tea and I feel more sleepy than ever. Right now I'm not real sure about the meaning of life.

## FEBRUARY 10

I want to awaken from my sleepwalking state.

I don't want to awaken just for a moment. I've done that before, and I'm sure it will happen again. It's wonderful—and it's not enough. "Peak experience." I'm not looking for peak experience. Up and then down again. What I want is a new plateau.

I don't want to be a star. I want to be a better human being happily lost in a world of better human beings.

Better = better functioning, more caring, more aware.

I like being here. I want to be more awake.

## FEBRUARY 11

It stands to reason that if one didn't like being here, one would want to be more asleep. More unconscious. More booze, more drugs, more material gratification. More TV. Less and less naked contact with nature, the moment, other people, one's self.

## FEBRUARY 12

Contact with other people can also be used to keep us asleep, but only if it isn't naked, isn't honest. What a lot of us like to do is pretend to be awake (so no one will bother us and we can go on sleeping). As an extension of this, we pretend to be honest. And we get so good at it, we fool ourselves.

If it's easy to tell the truth, you probably aren't being totally honest.

## FEBRUARY 13

People are learning to channel healing energy with their hands. Can we also learn to be honest with our hands, when our tongues and minds have themselves blocked or hopelessly tangled? Can we allow ourselves to be touched, knowing those hands can read the truth our minds and tongues so want to hide?

Ultimately we create what we want to create, communicate what we will to be communicated. But intention can be divided, and then the habit patterns of the instruments (mind, tongue) tend to determine the outcome. Conscious access to alternate instruments could tip the balance, away from self-protective habit patterns of long fearfulness and towards the honesty of our higher selves.

## FEBRUARY 14

A lot depends on what we imagine is possible. Is it possible for me to be loved? To be free of money anxieties? To be honest about my feelings?

Before asking what it takes for you to get what you want, ask first, what will it take for you to be able to *imagine* that this is possible? Put some energy into imagining it, work on the obstacles that come up. After you overcome the obstacles that keep you from being able to imagine it, other obstacles tend to fall away.

## FEBRUARY 15

For me, a big obstacle to imagining me having what I want is I'm so busy protecting myself from disappointment. I'd rather not have it than be disappointed. I'd rather not have a chance of having it, than be disappointed. I guess I don't want to be vulnerable. Somehow imagining having it makes me imagine thinking I'll have it and then not getting it, and I think I can't stand it. My imagination backfires, my mind overloads and the whole system breaks down.

What I notice is, I don't trust myself to be disappointed. I don't think I can handle it. I don't trust my ability to be in the moment.

I'm like an overprotective mother and an overprotected child wrapped up in the same person.

27

## FEBRUARY 16

I'm big enough to take disappointment. There. It's time I told myself that.

## FEBRUARY 17

Set your imagination free.

## FEBRUARY 18

My purpose is to touch other people by being myself. My purpose is to respond creatively to this situation I find myself born into. My power only feels like it's mine when I'm using it in service to something greater than me. Constantly in my life I drift away from that awareness and return to it. When I'm away, I spin my wheels, I reach for the moon and miss it, I wonder why I feel like a thief. When I return, I do great deeds and experience the satisfaction of being alive and being able. This is not a matter of right and wrong. It's only about what works for me. I get my satisfaction from knowing you want me and knowing I'm giving myself to you.

## FEBRUARY 19

I'm sweeping the floor. My sons have finished eating breakfast, they're getting dressed for school, I've made their box lunches and eaten some cereal myself and I start sweeping up the dining room and the phone rings, my friend Shirley has found a place for us to do a workshop in June, I say great, let's do it. Taiyo says goodbye to me and runs to catch the bus. I get off the phone and now Kenta is ready to go, he has his guitar and his lunch box, see you this afternoon. I finish sweeping the dining room and start on the kitchen. I stop to mix up some grapefruit juice and brewer's yeast. In a few minutes I'll start working on this book or type some more of Jules' book or write to Laura about promoting her father's writings. The fire radio goes off. Multiple car accident on Highway 12 (again!) at Dunbar Road. I'm still in pajamas. Throw on my overalls, grab some socks, I can't separate them, end up grabbing another pair, the rug is caught in the door, get the door closed and into the car and off to the fire station. I'm in the second truck. Messy accident, three cars, but no fatalities and apparently no very serious injuries. I end up directing traffic. Later I learn that my son's teacher was one of the people injured. An hour later, I get the mail on my way home from the station, there's a letter from the woman who brought me to Switzerland last fall to lead workshops, she's got some very important things to tell me, personal stuff, love, anger, and also she talks about our friend Judith, who I'm still in love with, mentions Judith leaving a club at 3 A.M. to go home with some man she just met, I'm all stirred up, haven't had a chance to read the letter carefully yet, just skimmed it, there's a message on my phone machine in the office from an old friend who also called yesterday and missed me, I called her back then and missed her, I decide the moment is now and call and we connect, we talk, feels good, feels like something will come of this, into the house with the letter from Switzerland and I realize that what I have to do is write this down, this feeling of how life just keeps coming at you, get up in the morning and let the tide bring the waves crashing over you and just flow with it, surrender, ride it, create with it, let yourself feel whatever you feel, be glad you don't live so far from the water that the waves can never touch you, it's better this way—oh yeah I called the school from the fire station to see if they needed a parent to come in and help the substitute teacher with the class, but they already had it covered—better to be in the middle of life wondering how you'll ever survive it than to be safely on the sidelines wondering how to get into the game. I'll go read that letter now.

## FEBRUARY 20

You could have asked me any time in the last ten years if I was a jealous person, and I would have said no. And I

29

would have thought I was telling the truth. But now, if I'm honest I have to admit I'm filled with irrational jealousy towards my children's mother (I have trouble thinking of her as my wife any more) and towards Judith (thought I'd let go of this stupid possessiveness, but apparently not). My mind rejects this double standard, I mean what's okay for me ought to be okay for my loved ones too. But my gut reaction is something else, and too strong to be denied. Not that I haven't denied it. But today my choice is to open my eyes and see my own insanity and shrug my shoulders and laugh and weep.

Just not wanting a feeling to be there doesn't make it go away.

Letting it be okay for it to be there is the only other tactic I can think of.

### February 21

In the midnight hour we meet again as strangers, free of the burdens of history. Wouldn't it be nice to slip away together to a place like that and not bring our memories with us?

### February 22

If I could forget who I thought you were, I know I'd be delighted to have you as you are in my life.

But who I thought you were is so precious to me, it seems I'm unwilling to let go of it now.

And that means, no matter how you look at it, that I'm not willing to let you be who you are.

Oh, I could say I'm willing, a thousand times, but truth reveals itself in spite of such claims. Indeed, the claims themselves can be a tip-off that something is wrong. Methinks the gentleman protesteth too much.

This state of not being able, or willing, to let you be exactly who you are, is not what I could call love. It's conditional. In effect I'm saying, "I'll love you if you do certain things, or if you conform to an image I have of you." That's not love.

Got myself cornered here. There's no way I want to admit it, but based on the evidence, this sounds like a case of adoration.

Did you ever have anybody adore you? Isn't it icky?

I am grateful to James Keys, who wrote the following lines in his book *Only Two Can Play This Game:* "We all adore or hate in another what we have alienated in ourselves. Adoration is not love, it is hatred in reverse."

Ten years ago, when someone was adoring me oppressively, those lines set me free. And now that I'm catching myself in the act, they hit me like a punch in the stomach.


## FEBRUARY 23

Funny thing. I hadn't thought of that book in years. Three weeks ago in Orange County, I was talking to a friend on the phone and she said, in an uncomfortable way, that this man adored her. Suddenly it all came back to me and I quoted the book to her as best I could from memory.

And oddly enough, later that same day I was at someone else's house and I happened to look at a small bookshelf in their living room and there was James Keys' book. It was the first copy I had seen in ten years.


## FEBRUARY 24

Isn't it funny how that voice inside says, "If I can't love her, I can't love anybody"? And all the time the truth is: Until I stop adoring her, I won't be able to love her or anyone else.

What have I alienated in myself? Well, the clue would be to ask, what is it I see in her? Oh. Oh God.

Beauty. Sexuality. Spontaneity. Intelligence. Spiritual power.

I'm not willing to let her be who she is, whoever that may be, because I'm not willing to let myself be who I am.

Uh, this has been very interesting. Can I change the subject now?

31

It's time to make dinner. I think I'll make spaghetti. And salad. I have this feeling I should make something else, but what else goes with spaghetti besides salad? French bread, I suppose, but I'm not that ambitious tonight. Well, it's kind of nice that I've joined the ranks of those who spend the day wondering what to make for dinner.

You know, I'm not really eager to change the subject. Love or adoration or whatever it is is such a delicious pain to indulge in. One can wallow in it indefinitely, pretending to suffer every inch of the way and enjoying it tremendously. It's kind of like being lazy, like the way I play solitaire over and over instead of going to answer the mail. Oh, rejected love, what could someday be, what might have been, such great places to hide from what is right now.

An empty stomach and two hungry boys will force me to make dinner. But what power on earth can force me to love in the present, instead of in the past and the future?

"Waking Up Together" was the title of a talk I gave to a half-dozen audiences, mostly in bookstores, in the spring of '82. The full title was "Waking Up Together: Life After Disarmament," and my intention was to point out the connection between planetary awakening and the anti-nuclear-weapons movement. When I speak, my audience often contains many people who've read *Das Energi*, so I took my title from a section of that book that describes the transition into collective consciousness, humankind as a single being, which includes the phrase, "we will all wake up together."

The thesis of my talk, I suppose, was that we keep talking about the next step of human evolution, the big leap, but it's kind of scary and we naturally put off actually letting ourselves get there. And I compare this to writing or any other task and mention the usefulness of having a deadline. Sometimes you have to force yourself, corner yourself, in order to transcend the hesitation and procrastination that keeps you from a desirable accomplishment. I do, anyway. And so the problem for the human species, ready for the next step and in real need but still damned reluctant, is: how do you corner yourself on a sphere?

And the answer is, stockpile a bunch of weapons that can blow up the sphere, and rig the whole thing so it's sure to go off unless we can make that breakthrough in awareness and communication.

Superbeing, the conscious biosphere, is waking up in the middle of the night to discover its house is on fire. That should get the old adrenalin going!

These are exciting times to be alive in.

Good morning.


### FEBRUARY 27

Imagine yourself on a boat. You are sailing out of a quiet bay and into the open ocean. The wind is with you and just strong enough, the sun is shining and you feel ready for anything.

A messenger arrives. No one knows exactly how he got there, but a man in a small motorboat is alongside the bow and coming on ship with an envelope in his hand. The envelope has your name written on it. The messenger says, "Your mother is dead." Inside the envelope is a sheet of paper with two numbers on it that you take to be longitude and latitude. You go below to look at your maps.


### FEBRUARY 28

"If you choose to go on this adventure," you tell the assembled crew, "please know we are sailing into the unknown. I cannot tell what will become of us."


### FEBRUARY 29

Then again you retire below to be alone with your feelings.

# Chapter Three

# MARCH

### MARCH 1

Is there anything I need to know before I begin? This is a philosophical question, really. I could apply it to the workshop I'm going to be leading on Friday. I often start by letting people introduce themselves, and asking them what it is they hope to get out of this experience. But that isn't something I need to know before I begin—at that point, the workshop has already begun. Whatever it is I do, I'm doing it. It wasn't necessary to collect any particular information first.

Is there anything I need to know before I begin this

chapter? Do I need to know what it will be about? Well, the truth is I have no way of knowing. I could have some ideas about what it will be about—okay if I have 'em, okay if I don't have 'em. It'll be whatever it turns out to be, regardless.

Is there anything I need to know before I start speaking out on the subject of disarmament? Many people would say so. Many people (for example) have said and do say that peace is a matter of arms control, and arms control must be left to the experts. The abysmal failure of the experts so far only means that the situation is getting more dangerous, and the more dangerous it is the more it is necessary, according to this argument, to let the experts handle it. In fact, it says here in the morning paper, if the people express their desire for peace that will greatly increase the chances of war, because it throws a monkey wrench into the experts' negotiations.

"Fear attacks the mind, it takes over, it starts calling the tune, after a while it looks like your friend, your protector. It tells you what to say and do so nothing scary will happen. If you don't obey, it scares you to prove its point."

Is there anything I need to know before I begin? Yes. I need to know that it's up to me, and no one else can begin for me. And then I need to make a choice.


## MARCH 2

The situation of our generation is this: we have woken up to find ourselves in bed with the Bomb.

This is not a pleasant situation, and it's not real obvious what to do about it.

What most of us do, faced with a nasty situation we can't get away from and to which there is no obvious appropriate response, is: we block out the information. There is no bomb in my bed, and anyway it has to be there or someone else would blow me up, and anyway it doesn't bother me, let's change the subject.

We deny the reality. We lie to ourselves, we "go into denial." In effect, when we wake up to bad news we think we can't handle, part of us goes to sleep again. So we live on a planet of sleepwalkers.

## MARCH 3

Tonight I feel much joy. The workshop is over and it went very very well. It is wonderful to have an experience of being good at what one does. And this work, when it goes well, is so much fun for me. It is a blessing.

## MARCH 4

And tonight, another night, I feel lost again. My health is not quite right. My phone won't stop ringing. I'd probably feel bad if it didn't ring, too. I'm thinking about the women in my life that I think I shouldn't be thinking about. I feel a need, a desire, to make progress in writing this book. And I'm making it difficult for myself.

And maybe all this is some kind of crazy sign that I'm on the right track. I'm working through something, and it's all coming out, like a sweat. The fact that I don't feel comfortable means something is really happening. And there's nothing to do but just let it all wash over me, and know it's all right to be here. And allow myself to do nothing.

## MARCH 5

If the struggle is to be all of who I am, who am I struggling against? Let's just say, for the sake of argument, that I am beautiful, sexy, spontaneous, intelligent, and full of spiritual power. And let's say I'm sitting here with a raging sore throat and a heart full of emptiness because I know I can have whatever I want if I'm willing to be who I am, and it scares me. I'm hesitating on the brink. I get sick in an effort to slow myself down.

I'm still in love with Judith. So what? Now listen: something very important about this mystery of men and women is, no matter how dead or asleep you are, a woman or a man can come along and wake you up, cut through all your resistance and defenses and leave you open to the world.

This is an extraordinary event. And fixating on the event is one of the subtle techniques we have for going back to sleep.

Another example: my friend Jules experienced a great awakening as a result of all-but-dying in an automobile accident. And it's just possible that his fascination with this event is actually a way of avoiding the effects of the event, that is, being fully awake in the moment. So that the car wreck becomes something outside himself he can relate to, the way he once related to his natural foods store.

Ultimately, then, he could use his "awakening" as an object around which to recreate all his old habit patterns, the ones he awakened from.

And I could turn my feelings for Judith into a refuge for my weakness, instead of allowing them to be a source for my strength. All I have to do to do this is focus on the past and the possible future, instead of the present.

And her very importance to me (the importance of what happened and what could happen) becomes my excuse for focusing on the past or the future.

Or I could sit here in a stupor waiting for another woman to come along and waken me again, becoming as it were addicted to the experience, falling asleep repeatedly because it feels so good to wake up.

Or: I could admit that I am what I saw in her, and what she saw in me, I could treasure the love that I feel for her now, and give it away to the world. I could let go of everything I think I want, and surrender to the will of God.


MARCH 6

The subject of this book is, being in the moment. So I would like to be able to write about anything that's happening, whatever's here at the moment that I write. And right now I notice I don't feel comfortable telling you about my arguments with my younger son.

It is very frustrating to tell Taiyo to do anything, and there are a lot of things he needs to be told. He needs to be told not to rub his eyes with his dirty hands. He needs to be told to blow his nose. (He's eight years old . . . and yes I know there are a lot of other eight-year-olds the same.) Just now he needed to be told to wear a hat or a coat with a hood when it's raining.

And instead of going in to get a hat, he started to argue with me about it. That's what's frustrating. And what's especially frustrating is how angry he makes me, and what a trap it is (doing neither of us any good).

Like many children, he is relatively obedient at school and at other people's houses. But he frequently resists doing what his father or mother ask him to do, because the request or command seems unreasonable or just because he doesn't want to do it. Probably at first he doesn't want to make the effort or interrupt (or stop) what he's doing, and then after that it becomes a matter of not wanting to give you the satisfaction of his obedience, not wanting the other person to "win." And one thing that's frustrating is I get caught up in the same emotions. I don't want him to win. There's an emotional side to this, and also a rational one: I believe that letting the child win (he ends up not having to clean up his room right now, even though you told him to) teaches him that this tactic of resistance works at least some of the time, and therefore encourages him to keep doing it.

But I don't like the way my anger traps me.

Maybe I can learn to let go of my anger without letting go of the issue. How to provide firm guidelines without leaning on or falling into anger—this has been and probably will be a challenge for me throughout my life as a parent.


MARCH 7

Writing that last section was not as hard (or painful, or embarrassing) as I thought it would be. So often the anticipation is worse than the act. If we could only remember this, perhaps we would find it easier to gain the benefits of telling the truth in the moment.

39

## MARCH 8

The more scared and reluctant you feel, the more probable value there is in saying what you don't want to say.

It is easy, and valuable, to come from enthusiasm. It is difficult, and just as valuable, to come from reluctance.

## MARCH 9

A "belief" is an assumption that is so automatic with us that we don't even know it's there. Many of our daily actions are controlled or affected by our beliefs. And by definition, acting out of a belief (whether the belief is "right" or "wrong") is the opposite of being in the moment.

Last night before I fell asleep I suddenly recognized a very powerful belief (often referred to as a "core belief") that I have about anger. I realized that when I'm angry, something inside me automatically and absolutely believes that the fact of my anger means the other person has done something wrong.

The result of this is that even when it's pointed out to me (or I spontaneously notice) that there's no reason to be angry, or that my reaction is out of proportion, I stay angry anyway. Often my mind quickly grabs at *another* reason for anger (something saved up for just such an occasion, or perhaps invented on the spot). Sometimes I'll notice myself doing this, and still not be able to stop it—it's frustrating, it feels like my anger is out of control.

Yes. The reason it's so hard for me to shut off my anger, the reason it feels out of the control of my conscious mind, is that I'm responding to something deeper and more powerful than my conscious mind: a core belief that says, if I'm angry, I've goddamn well got a *reason* to be angry! The person I'm angry at must have done something, or I wouldn't be feeling this way!

This core belief of mine happens to be untrue. I know all too well that sometimes (often) my anger is unjustified, or out of proportion. But notice that it doesn't matter whether a belief is true or not! What is destructive is the fact that re-

40

sponse to the belief is automatic, overriding other considerations and making it impossible for us to respond to what's actually happening. We respond to our beliefs instead.

That's why the important thing to do with a belief is: *know that it's there*. Changing and revising our beliefs is fine as far as it goes, but it never goes to the heart of the problem. Identifying and being aware of our beliefs is the only way to avoid being controlled by them, moment to moment.

You have to know there's an automatic override—if you don't know that, or you don't know what it is, there's no way you can reach in and shut it off in an emergency.

As you uncover your basic beliefs, don't put all your energy into trying to change them. All you'll get is a new set of problems. Instead, put your energy into maintaining awareness of what those beliefs are—and know that, with this knowledge, at any given moment you can choose not to be controlled by them.

### MARCH 10

Don't try to choose right now, once and forever. It won't work. Human freedom depends on choosing anew every moment.

### MARCH 11

We don't trust our future selves. We want to get everything worked out now, so our future selves won't be able to make any mistakes. It's like, I'm feeling clear right now, and I want to *make sure* I don't make a mess of things or get confused again in the future. So I'll just install this little safety device, and make absolutely sure it can't be turned off or interfered with—

Today's understanding is tomorrow's trap. Understand it . . . and let go of it.

You say you don't trust yourself. Maybe you'll forget. The truth is, you won't forget. But if you do, that's better than locking yourself into remembering.

41

How do you like being controlled by your past self?
Okay, so give your future self a break.


## MARCH 12

Three minutes to midnight, the day after we've gone into
Daylight Savings Time and no one knows what time it really
is: I've been sitting around talking with an old friend about
people and situations and interests of ours that few other
people on earth know anything of or could ever appreciate.
Feels good, giving both of us a chance to really stretch those
parts of our identities, let them out into the sunlight for a
few hours (then back they go to the memory pits, deep in
the caves of attention).

I promise you, whoever you are, there's someone or
some place that you and I both know that we could sit down
and have a great old time talking about, if we would just
allow ourselves the opportunity to do that.

We are connected. It wouldn't be half so much fun to be
alone here if it weren't that there's other people alone here
too.


## MARCH 13

Friendship is a comfort all the more treasured by those
who are constantly diving into the unknown, alone.


## MARCH 14

In these international days, I am pleased to be a voice,
however feeble, who is heard in more than one nation and
culture. It tickles me that I'll be published soon in Switzerland, India and Israel. And I'm very proud of my Japanese
lady-friend who is singing in English in Germany. This is the
direction to go in. Let's build these bridges. As Sachiko says
in one of her songs, "let's have communication."

Let's speak, sing, listen, smile. And dance.

## March 15

For me, this current great awakening involves:
choosing to be stewards of this earth and all that lives on it;
choosing to move away from rather than towards nuclear holocaust;
and choosing to be aware of and to defend the rights of all human beings everywhere.

And how we do it is: self-awareness, self-reliance, interpersonal and international communication, "getting in touch with one's individual power," being in the moment, telling the truth in public, transmitting healing energy and love.


## March 16

These are the basic rights that belong to any human being, no matter where that person lives, no matter who he or she is:
* The right to life, liberty, and security of person
* Freedom from torture or cruel, inhuman treatment or punishment
* Freedom from hunger
* Freedom of opinion and expression, freedom of information
* The right to work, and to choose one's own employment
* Freedom from arbitrary arrest, detention, or exile
* The right of association and assembly
* The right to move freely within each country, and the right to leave any country, including one's own
* The right to return to one's own country
* The right of equal pay for equal work
* The right to marry and found a family, to equal rights in marriage and freedom from forced marriage
* Freedom of thought, conscience and religion
* Freedom from slavery and servitude
* The right of privacy

43

★ The right to own property

★ The right to a standard of living adequate for health and well-being (including food, clothing, housing, medical care)

★ The right to equal protection of the law, equality before the law, and recognition as a person before the law

★ The right to participate in government, the right of free elections

★ The right to special care and assistance for the elderly, the handicapped, for mothers, and for all children

★ The right to education, and the rights of parents to choose the kind of education given to their children

★ The right to effective judicial remedy, the right to a fair trial, the right to be presumed innocent until proven guilty

★ The right to form and join trade unions

★ The right to a nationality, the right of asylum

★ The right to rest and leisure

★ The right to a world that works for everyone

### March 17

The most important step towards universal respect for these basic rights is for all people on earth (as many as possible) to know that these are their rights, and that there is agreement among human beings that these are the rights of all of us.

Many of these rights are at present routinely denied to individuals in all parts of the world. Universal awareness of these rights, and universal awareness that agreement has been reached that these rights belong to every one of us, is the essential ingredient in improving the present situation. Spreading this awareness is direct action on behalf of every individual human on the planet.

### March 18

I'm on the road again, got a lot to say one moment, total fog the next, no correcting typewriter in the familiar

44

comfort of my home to sit down at, plenty of distractions, and I'm trying to find my voice. Ahem, ahem. Talk about the midnight hour—I finally reunited with a woman and soul partner I haven't seen since the night we met almost four years back, and it was like not a minute had passed. And that as much as anything I suppose (and the nearness of having just been with her, those moments when life is so full, so hot) has me all turned upside down again. I feel like I've just been through a great healing. Or else I've been ripped open.

She was telling me on Sunday about the tiny town in California she grew up in. And the very next day that goddamn town was thoroughly destroyed by an earthquake.

I'm not making this stuff up you know.


## MARCH 19

Yes I'm excited about life, about the possibilities. No. The actualities. I've been excited about possibilities way too long. And I don't need them any more. (Got to remind myself of that.) What is actual is enough.

Enough? It's too much! It's overflowing, I can't handle it, I don't know what to do with all this feeling, and that's why I want to retreat into possibilities. What is here and now is too wonderful, I'm afraid of it, I don't know how to calm down.

Or, it's just a habit, to make possibilities, to project my excitement into the future. And knowing that, I can balance it by stopping my mind (letting go of it) and just being here with my feelings now.

I'm learning to love people in the present, without possibilities. And I'm learning to let the excitement be here. And I'm learning, ever so slowly, to love myself in the present, and let the possibilities fall where they may.


## MARCH 20

I would like to be able to articulate, in the form of a 25-30 minute talk, my ideas about how the changes we'd like to see in our world can come about, and how you and I can make the difference in this process by choosing to use our own power. The talk should be short to leave as much time as possible for questions and interaction. Speaking to people can open doors, but interacting with people is what really gets results. How can I do it in such a way that each of you will know I'm talking to *you* and not some other allegedly more powerful person?

I don't want to just give a rousing performance of words we've all heard before. I'd rather work in the area of things we've probably said to ourselves but that are seldom or never said out loud or in public. And as you've noticed, I enjoy combining ingredients that aren't usually found together.

Those of us who are even conscious of having a collective or public purpose usually find it at odds with our private purpose, or else we experience that one tends to greatly overshadow the other (public issues to excess for a few years, then retreat into private goals, or vice versa). My observation is that this is a trick of perception, and that it is always possible to bring these seemingly different sides of ourselves together, for the benefit of both. I wrote in my pamphlet *Common Sense,* "Today I take a vow, not to love the world more than myself, not to love myself more than I love the world." Like any vow it must be acted on every day. And it can be done.

Notice how the things I'm saying don't quite seem to come together. That's the challenge of my talk: to make it all *seem* to come together just enough to have the impact I want, one person hearing what she needs to hear and someone else hearing what he needs to hear, each person finding something of real value without being able to distract themselves with the game of criticism and argument. I don't need agreement, and I even welcome disagreement as long as it doesn't interfere with each person's hearing and connecting with the tidbit that will make a difference for them at this moment. In fact I prefer that we all move in our different ways; as long as we're *moving,* I know that we're moving together. Perhaps I'll rephrase that: as long as we're acting from our hearts.

My purpose as a speaker is to inspire people to act from their hearts. Sometimes my words could be a stimulus for this; but the same words must also be willing and able to serve as a simple distraction. The words distract the minds of the listeners, and allow their hearts to be present. And in that moment those hearts feel not me so much as the energy of all those other hearts in the room that are longing to be fulfilled and take loving action.

Each listener awakens in different ways, at different moments, yet we share an experience of waking up together. And this experience gives us courage to go on.

### MARCH 21

I'm not in love with Judith any more. I do and can feel a lot of love for her, but it's not the same. I guess it means I'm not longing for her any more. "In love" sometimes seems a very powerful illusion of helplessness.

And I think I'm not angry at my wife any more, either. Oh, freedom.

And I've lost nothing. "In love" is only a kind of obsession. The end of obsession is like an unclenching of emotional muscles. I can relax. And who she is, and who I am, and whatever the relationship between us may be, all remain unchanged.

### MARCH 22

Isn't it funny, how time heals wounds? If you let it. I mean, it helps not to pick at the scabs every day.

### MARCH 23

"When I get this feeling," says Marvin Gaye, "I need sexual healing." Very true. And by extension, I make love with and am healed by everything that exists in my universe.

### MARCH 24

We cannot consciously enter the midnight hour. We can

put ourselves in favorable circumstances: go to Carnival, or a convention; listen to the right music; spend time alone with a friend. But there is no technique for getting from here to there. It's not an objective place. "At what time will I next experience being outside of time?" The question has no answer.

## MARCH 25

All right now, let's break free.

I have before me two books. One is a first novel just published this month. By page 20, I wasn't sure if I liked it. By page 40 I had decided to buy three copies—tomorrow— one for myself, and at least two to give or loan to friends. (The copy I'm reading is on loan from some friends of the author—perhaps the book is not even on sale yet.)

The other book was published in 1954, as far as I can tell. It is a "Modern Library" paperback (the first I can remember seeing) of 180 drawings by Picasso, done consecutively from 28 Nov. '53 to 3 Feb. '54. There is an introduction by Rebecca West, who just died this year. The book belongs to my father's wife—I found it among her excellent collection of art books. (I am visiting their house in Seattle.) It is wonderful, extraordinary! And it reminds me of how chance brought me the opportunity to see a similar set of Picasso drawings at the Bridgestone Museum in Tokyo two years ago, just after I first became interested in Picasso. My wife was with me then, sharing my enthusiasm. I'd like her to see this book.

## MARCH 26

I wrote the previous section so that you could see another side of me.

By the way, the novel is *Tea with the Black Dragon,* by R. A. MacAvoy.

## March 27

I am a reader too (though I feel like I read damn little), not only a writer. I am a listener as well as a speaker. And I have an almost uncontrollable desire to express my enthusiasm, put it in words—and share my likes with other people. This is sheer vanity. But perhaps it is a socially beneficial vanity, like wearing beautiful clothes.

All I know is, I need a receptacle for all this joy that boils up inside me.

Thank you for the space you've given me.

## March 28

Picasso is as outrageously, forthrightly sexual as the young man who made my favorite album of the moment, a black Minnesota musician named Prince. The album is from a couple of years ago, and it's called *Dirty Mind:*

> There's something about you babe
> Happens every time
> Everyone around you babe
> They get a dirty mind . . .

Sex seems to be important in my life right now. I don't know why I like this album but it turns me on in dozens of ways. I listened to 20 different cassettes driving up from San Francisco, and this is the only one I've wanted to hear again and again.

*Picasso and the Human Comedy* is the name of that paperback. It's delicious.

## March 29

Something else that's important to me, that I find in Picasso and Prince and other people and writings/creations that are attractive to me right now, is humor. God, it feels good to laugh!

## March 30

Bad news is no excuse for the suppression of laughter. Often that's when we need it most.

To me it is the height of sanity to know how bad things are in Guatemala, to feel it and open oneself and respond, take action—and to go on enjoying laughter and orgasms, not at the same moment but perhaps the same day. Same goes for personal bad news. Of course, this is a standard of sanity that I don't always live up to. Sometimes I'm crazy enough to believe that punishing myself will help me serve other people.

## March 31

There is a bomb in my bed. But there's still room for you, my friend.

# Chapter Four

# APRIL

### April 1

In six days I will be thirty-five years old. Seven years ago I was powerfully struck by the fact that Bob Dylan's live album *Hard Rain,* to me one of his most passionate, energetic, life-filled performances on record, was recorded the night before his thirty-fifth birthday. "What are you going to say," I wrote in a review at the time, "now that you've looked and seen that burning intensity, that passionate youthful energy we supposedly lost with the 1960s, on the face of a 35-year-old millionaire? You've either got to deny the existence of passion altogether (a popular stance), or else admit that your own life might not be over yet."

Last fall I finally shaved the beard I'd worn for a dozen years. Couple of months later I suddenly cut through the Gordian knot of my marriage (it was only my own *ideas* about the relationship that were limiting me, I see now, and they limited me because I wanted and needed them to, so I wouldn't have to face my own power). Not long after that my wife left for three months in Europe with her music and her boyfriend, and a couple of days later I began writing this book. Now in six days she returns. I don't think I'll stop writing.

I don't think I'll grow my beard back.

My life's not over yet.


### APRIL 2

Am I too personal? No, I don't think so, and I'll tell you why. Every book I write, like every song the singer sings and every painting the painter paints, says the same thing; but each one says it a different way, and so (as Picasso for example paints his guitars, bulls, owls and women's faces, over and over) the universe is embraced. Today my subject is your personal power, the fact (perceived by me as a fact) that you have as much power to influence the fate of the world as the current U.S. president or Soviet premier or any other person or set of people you care to name. I also have this power and am by God doing my best to exercise it. Hearing this, you might suppose that I would give up sex and science fiction and money worries and walks in the woods, and focus on the Big Issues of the Day. But that's not the point. I draw my power from being who I am, not from trying to live up to some image of what I imagine the exercise of power would look like.

You give up nothing when you choose to exercise your power. On the contrary, you expand, embracing all the aspects of who you are and letting go of your need to pretend to be somebody different. You don't have to be perfect to have an effect on the universe. What would help is to let go of the feeling that first you have to be perfect and then you can take action.

You are having an effect on the universe right now. If your belief is that first you have to do A (get some money to go to art school) before you can do B (paint a pretty picture), then you personally are the one who's causing the universe to hang out in a state of I'm-not-ready. Meanwhile you get older and the universe decays entropically and the air seems to fill with anxiety about when this elusive readiness will arrive and whether or not it will be Too Late. And the thickness in the air makes you almost want to give up the whole game. Meanwhile, whether you realize it or not, other beings are breathing your side-smoke.

Don't misunderstand. There's absolutely nothing to feel guilty about, because you are doing a perfect job of being yourself at this moment. This beautiful universe we live in today is entirely your creation. What I want to do is speak to that part of you that aspires and desires, and let you know that if there's something you really want (whether it sounds like something totally personal, like a trip to Paris, or totally collective, like planetary survival) you have the power to create it. And all the tools you need to do the job are already in your kit, and there's nobody anywhere who can get in your way. You have the power, and you exercise it by keeping in mind what you really want, and letting yourself be yourself.

I know—you're afraid of your power—so am I of mine, very much so. That's why we have so much trouble trying to use our power to get what we think we want. (You think you want money to go to art school.) (But you don't really want money, so you can't be totally yourself and use your true power in the effort to get it. Some people really want money, and they get it, effortlessly, but you're not one of them. Recognize that what you really want is to paint a pretty picture. You'll find that all you have to do is choose to do it, and when you're coming from what you really want you're bigger than all your fears.)

Your fears are not illusions. You have excellent reasons, based on personal experience, to be afraid of your own power. Maybe you hurt someone else with it. Certainly you got hurt yourself. Going for what you really want won't get rid of your fears or eliminate the dangers, but it will give you the courage you need to take action anyway. Using your power to get what you really want in spite of the risks and the fears is true courage; it is expressing who you really are; it is expressing your love.

I need to be just as personal in this book as I find myself being. This is the song I can sing at this moment. I could try to sing some other song—based on my fears about what I "should" be doing and what I might imagine you want from me—but neither of us would be happy with the results. Let me put it this way: to be consistent with my own teachings and in order to come from my power, I have to let you see who I am.

This is fun. I know what I'm doing. I'm pretending that it might be all right to be who I really am.

### APRIL 3

This might be a silly analogy, but here goes: when I'm driving around, I encounter both stoplights and stop signs. A stoplight says, "stop until I say go." We stop; we wait; when it tells us to go, we go. A stop sign says, "stop, look around, then go when it's safe to go."

Seems what I and a lot of us do in our lives is, we spend years and years hanging out at stop signs waiting for them to turn green.

"Stop" doesn't always mean stop forever, or stop till I tell you to go. Very often it means, "stop and look and then go when it's time to go." But we get confused and we stop and stay stopped, stay stuck in our same old positions.

Waiting for a message that never comes; waiting for someone else to set us free.

### APRIL 4

You don't have to sit there and be miserable, my friend. You don't have to sit there and be bored. You don't have to sit there and be worried. You can go on with your life now.

## APRIL 5

This desk is a mess. My life is not a mess. Actually, that's pretty good, isn't it? It would be much worse to have a clean desk and a messed-up life.

I went to another auto accident this evening. This guy had slammed his truck into a tree so hard it's amazing there was anything left of him at all, but somehow he was alive and conscious and I was holding his head (we put on a C-collar to keep the neck rigid) and holding his back so he didn't try to get up while other firemen were checking his legs (several bad open fractures) and pulling back the seat with a chain so we could get him out of there without further damage. The paramedics arrived. I kept talking to the guy. I don't know what happened (how he hit the tree) but a number of people know him and someone said the way he's been drinking lately it was just a matter of time. I guess I can tell you that, you don't know what day this is or even what town. Young guy. Killing yourself by drinking is really rotten, considering how easy it is to take innocent bystanders with you. The weird thing is, people do it because it's socially acceptable—more so than pills, say. Real men don't overdose on barbiturates. They go out and get smashed and smash their pickups into trees. I say it's rotten 'cause I've seen their victims. On another level it's just a piece of this place and century, other places and times people did the same thing in some different ways. Anyway I hope this guy makes it, I think he will. I was cradling his head and talking to him just like his mother.

## APRIL 6

There was a concert at school tonight. My son plays guitar, he's in the fourth grade. I was late making dinner because I was talking on the phone with a guy who doesn't want me (my publishing company) to put out a new printing of his book. He'd rather I sold it to this other publisher, even if we lose a bunch of money doing so, because it allows him the fantasy that the other publisher will launch a brilliant new promotion and make the book a big success. The truth is, I know exactly how he feels.

Anyway I rushed dinner. And also I'd been outside cutting the grass, and in my office vacuuming the cobwebs, I guess I'm trying to get the place clean before my wife comes home, for obscure reasons of my own (when I frantically try to clean up the place, it's not to be kind to the folks who are coming, it's all about my own self-image, the way I see me through others' eyes)—and I had one boy taking a shower while the other raked up weeds—we went to the concert, came home bought laundry soap started the wash I gave them some ice cream and they brushed teeth and put on pajamas and had just got to bed when the fire radio went off (that truck accident I told you about), they're old enough to be left on their own now, I guess I came back an hour or an hour and a half later. They were asleep, I compulsively went to my office to do more vacuuming. My wife's coming home, we need another place for one of us to live, but I'm not sure how fast that'll happen, meanwhile I've been writing in the house 'cause I've had a lot of privacy, got to clean the office to the point that I can feel comfortable writing and sleeping out there (it's a garage in back of the house, also the home of the publishing business, lots of books, boxes, file folders). And came in after 11:00 to call my friend Fax. She's an important romantic figure in my life right now, and also she said something in a letter about wanting to put on a workshop with me in Oregon, and I thought it would be easier to talk about it by phone than in letters.

I think I'm getting ready to say something about men and women. And I also have this feeling that maybe I won't say it. This book is getting away from me. I feel shy. Fax told me on the phone she felt a little guilty about feeling shy with me the last time we were together. I said being shy can be very attractive.

I know she likes me. That means a lot. I met another gal who likes me so much it's scary, I guess when people like you too much too easily it's hard to be sure it's you they really like. And also I could feel uneasy because I'm not sure if I like her the same much. But with Fax, there's balance, right at the moment. I can feel it. Or anyway I want it to be true. And I like her a lot. And the me she likes is really me, and I like the way her presence brings it out in me. And most of all, I like having romance in my life.


### April 7

I've been home for hours and I just looked in the mirror and I've got somebody else's blood on my face.


### April 8

Happy birthday to me. My wife's plane arrives in twelve hours. Now I feel like an actor, studying the script of my life. What's my motivation in this next scene? Love? Jealousy? Righteousness? Self-sacrifice?

Being in the moment means you don't get to rehearse the script ahead of time. All you can do is improvise.


### April 9

I'm scared and I'm tense and my mind says there's no reason to be so my response to that is to pretend that everything's fine with me. I tell myself I don't feel scared or tense, and I believe it. And meanwhile I'm just as scared and as tense as ever, and everybody knows it but me.

Only by being honest with myself, only by acknowledging my fear and my tension, can I give myself the space to choose not to act in a tense or fearful way.

By acknowledging the reality that's here and allowing ourselves to feel what we really feel, we make it possible to choose our actions consciously. And yet so much of the time we feed ourselves false information, about the way we think we should be instead of the way we are.

I love myself. And my last words before I fall asleep this early morning are: I want to have a relationship with myself that's based on honesty and trust.

APRIL 10

*Men and Women*

Dear A——,

Thank you for your letter I received this morning, the poem about you looking in the mirror and seeing my eyes. I can feel that you care about me very much. I know that sometimes I feel impatient, you're very pretty and you have a nice body and I'd like to put my arms around you and feel free to play together all night and run away and drive across America together and go dancing in rock and roll clubs in towns where no one knows us. I'm impatient to make love with you, to tell the truth.

I could end this letter with that last sentence, and send it to you, and I flatter myself that you'd probably be moved, be aroused, and even be tempted for a moment to kick everything over and run off to spend a night or a lifetime with me. Or maybe not. But if you were tempted . . .

I want to say, even if you did want to, for just a moment, of course you wouldn't do it. And then I'd list the obvious reasons: the man you're living with, your love for him and not wanting to hurt him or lose him, his importance in your life; your daughter, and what's good for her; etc. Or put it another way: I can feel that this is not the right moment in your life to rush off on a romantic adventure. Part of you might like to . . . and that part is probably not your superior person, as the *I Ching* says.

And from what I know about you, and what I know about life, there will be times (as there have been before), when it furthers the superior person to run off on a romantic adventure. I hope I'm around and available and attractive to you when that moment comes.

If I sent you the first paragraph of this letter only, I think you'd be flattered but also you'd feel uncomfortable, it would put you under pressure to respond, to say yes or no or to refuse to say, all of which could cause problems. And "problems" have the potential to increase the distance between us, or to close doors that are quietly open, and that's not what I want.

The best thing, I think, is to practice patience in the face of my own impatience. And to admit that I'm not so head-over-heels in love with you that I'm willing to throw all caution to the winds. So it's not just you that's not ready, that's slowing us down. I've got my own uncertainty and unreadiness, that I try hard to pretend isn't there; I'm not ready to kick everything over myself. We're both in this relationship together; I create it being the way it is right now just as much as you do . . . which is 100%. The way things are (for me) is 100% my creation, an expression of what I want, and what I'm willing to have, at this moment; the way things are (for you) is 100% your creation, an expression of what you want right now. That's the rule.

And it's possible that you know I'm impatient, when I think of you, to be with you and feel your arms around me, and therefore you also know that I'm practicing patience, because I respect you and your needs and what you're doing and because I want you enough to be willing to wait for our moment . . . and you can feel this, and feel the love in it, and that's something to treasure right now. I know I treasure your messages of love and caring for me, some of which clearly require real courage, and that also touches me and makes me feel you right now. This, not some future dream, is our relationship—and according to the rule, we're creating it this way because right now this is what we want.

I guess the desire itself, and the experience of mutual loving patience and courage, is what I want right now. Is it all right with you, that I'm not ready to come and push aside all my considerations and politeness and carry you away in my arms?

Love is the strangest thing. And I do love you, and I'm glad to have you in my life.

                                        Paul


**April 11**

Dear V——,

My mind has been chattering away since you called the other night. I don't think you quite realize it, but it feels like you're so excited about me that you can't see, hear, or feel me . . . which is a real no-win situation for both of us. And what really gets me is that I've been in your shoes so many times, have done that this very year, could probably do it again next month. So in a way it's great for me (very frustrating, but very valuable) to have the tables turned this way, to see things from the other side.

You saw me on Friday night, and decided to (try to) seduce me. You set up a radio interview with me for Sunday night, just caught me before I left town, it was a great conversation-on-tape and in addition you achieved your primary objective. I didn't have time, but your openness and honesty and unselfconscious headstrong determination and gorgeous face caused me and allowed me to create time where there was none, and we collided with sparks in the midnight hour.

I was flattered and charmed and stimulated and satiated, and looked forward to seeing you again whenever that might be. (A thousand miles is a fair distance, but both of us do get around, and life is long.) And then came your letter, followed by phone calls, communicating that I (or your idea of me) had instantly become so important in your life that now you desperately need reassurance.

You want to hear that I've created as intense a fantasy around you. And I haven't. And even if I had, experience tells me that that's not the road to a successful relationship. Mutual fantasy does lead to powerful entanglement and much rapid heartbeat, followed by a 99.9% probable outcome of crash-and-burn. But don't be confused. I'm not saying that therefore I've carefully chosen not to fall in love with you. I haven't really chosen anything. It just hasn't happened.

You put me in a position where I'm a cad if I don't tell you what you want to hear, and a liar if I do (and a cold son-of-a-bitch if I try to be reasonable about it, as I'm doing now). Well, I've put many a fine lady in the same position, and turnabout is fair play. But how can I tell you that I'm not rejecting you, just trying to give myself room to breathe so I won't have to reject you? As it stands, just seeing you again would be like leading you on.

I do appreciate your honesty and self-awareness. And like I say, I can easily see myself in your shoes. But that doesn't give me the solution to the riddle. You even let me know you feel jealous of a woman I haven't yet kissed. I know how strong these emotions can be, but they're hardly what I need or want in my life right now.

Maybe this is just your way of pushing me away as fast as you pulled me in. I surrendered before and I surrender now. I feel sorry to be misunderstood, but that is certainly a risk I took. I guess all I want to say is: you're sweet. I care about you. Slow down. I don't know how it's done, but I do know obsession must be conquered in oneself before there's any hope of getting to or getting back to love. Let's meet again on neutral ground, when you're ready, and find out who we are to each other.

Love,

Paul

### April 12

Oh gosh. I don't think all this honesty is going to win me many friends. It's helpful to the book, I suppose, and that's important; and actually it's helpful to me, kind of therapeutic, I get a chance to see things more clearly. But it's going to be embarrassing to let my other lovers read it (yeah I've got a few more; ain't single life exciting?). And I wonder at the effect on the intimacy between you and me, dear reader. Do you think I'm too easy? It's funny: my point of view is just the opposite. I feel like I've spent far too many years of my creative life playing hard to get.

### April 13

Actually none of what you read here is true. It's all a work of fiction. It's a novel about the thoughts that go through a person's head while waking up one spring morning in the late twentieth century.

## April 14

And he's trying to remember this dream about the midnight hour.

## April 15

Waking up. You know, when I chase you I imagine ecstasy; when you chase me I imagine loss of freedom. But when we're actually waking up together none of that matters, and maybe even they're both the same thing. I surrender, God. I'm willing to admit that this is the universe I'm choosing, and I wouldn't have it any other way than the way it is.

## April 16

My friend Peggy says we're not here to be spiritual. She says the point is that we *are* spirits, who chose to come here to experience being human.

We are always infinite. What's special about the moment is that it allows us to forget infinity and discover the joys of limitation.

## April 17

Birth and death are the limits, the edges of our lives. They make all this other stuff possible.

I like the part in Castaneda's books where Don Juan talks about Death as an ally. He says your personal death is always with you, a fleeting shadow hovering just out of line-of-sight on your lefthand side. Be aware of it, know that it's there, use it as a strength. It will help you to be in the moment.

## April 18

And what does all this have to do with the threat of

nuclear annihilation? Simply this: acknowledge that it's there. Let it motivate us to be who we can be, together; not some-day soon, but now.

## April 19

We give up nothing when we choose to exercise our power. We are having an effect on the universe right now. We don't have to sit here and be worried. We can choose our own future.

We can acknowledge the danger, and choose something more interesting for ourselves and our children than nuclear holocaust. All we need is a little confidence—or just some bravado, I mean we could always fake it—and just a dash of imagination.

## April 20

Nuclear annihilation is our friend, it's always with us, it reminds us that we came here for a reason.

We can go on with our lives now.

## April 21

Dear F——,

In a few hours, soon as I take another nap and S. gets home to be with the kids, I'm taking off on a long drive north to be with you and M. I'm pleased with myself, that I managed to make this choice out of all the possibilities confronting me. I know already no matter what happens it's the right thing to do at this moment.

My relationship with a certain kind of beauty seems to be to keep it at arm's length (or slightly further) or go into obsession. Now I think I'm choosing not to go into my automatic response. Which means I'm choosing to have the courage to let things be what they are. I'm curious to know what the world looks like when I'm not forcing myself to see it the way I think it should look.

I notice I'm talking to myself now, instead of to you. I know you don't mind, but isn't it funny that I should feel shy about talking to you? Well, uh, I guess it's what's happening. Anyway, there is something I want to tell you, and it has to do with what I wrote for April 19.

You are a very powerful person, and in some ways and much of the time you're in touch with your power, but you have great doubts about its value. Let me quote you from your wonderful story about Ana Sarka: "I just don't have it . . . I want to dissipate, entertain, move in circles of brilliant witty people. I want to be a writer, but I don't want to write! I finally realized that the only thing I do well, that I've perfected and made an art out of, is falling in love. It's like ritualized Kabuki theater. The hands come up, delicately curved, the eyes meet, lines are spoken, love walks on stage, and the players have leave to exit their minds."

You are a great performer, from the heart, on paper sometimes, on stage always. And since love is your message, love is your highest art. And perhaps, as the quote suggests, the initiation of love is your specialty. Well fine. What I want to tell you is, the world has great need of your talents.

Today, when we have real doubts about the existence of posterity, is hardly the time to write for posterity. If the fate of the earth indeed hangs in the balance (and it's our mutual vanity to believe that it does), then surely we want to use our talents to influence the choices that the peoples of the earth collectively make right now.

And, as you and M. and I have discussed before, we cannot influence them through anger and righteousness. It doesn't work. The way to reach them, to reach us, reach ourselves, is through the very gifts that you radiate when you allow yourself to be powerful: seduction, spontaneity, immediacy, love.

April 19 says that our greatest collective need is to start imagining a better future for ourselves than catastrophe and apocalypse. We need to be *inspired* to use our imaginations. We need you. In the moment, of the moment, whatever audience you find yourself before, do your dance of inspiration, sweet Fax (oops I said your name); sing your sparrow heart out. Make us fall in love with ourselves.

Inspire us to wake up together. That little art of falling in love can create in us the confidence to go out and choose new life, new worlds, new visions. I don't want to scare you, but I know who you really are, and I'm on my knees begging you to come back and help us in our time of need. And have fun doing it!

All love,
Paul

## April 22

A moment ago I was lying face down in the sun on the beautiful Oregon Dunes. I'm alone with hundreds of yards of warm clean fine sand around me in every direction—and patches of trees, and beach grass and ocean in the distance. I find myself here unexpectedly—spontaneously—it's wonderful!! This is the sand of my Cape Cod childhood summers. And it's different, too. I've never been here before. And yet I have. This is the sand of my dreams.

## April 23

Earlier today I napped for two hours on the soft floor of a redwood forest.

I'm writing in a small notebook usually used to keep mileage records in the car.

My sleeping bag is full of redwood needles, and my sweater is full of sand.

## April 24

I think I'm learning to be young and free again.

## April 25

This is a very wonderful world we live in. Tom Verlaine

sings, "When I/see the glory,/I ain't/got a worry." Yes. Without getting denominational, that says a great deal about my relationship with God.

Thank you, oh You-whom-I-thank, for letting me see the glory again.

### APRIL 26

I forget every day. This makes me a sleepwalker at times; but it also allows me the joys of rediscovery, remembering.

### APRIL 27

Now I remember you. How lovely to find you here . . .

### APRIL 28

"You" are Goddess, you are God, you are reader, audience, lover, friend—you are the other who is separate, apart, and therefore available for union. We must be apart to come together. I remember you. You are the one who stimulates me, wakes me up, the very thought of whom motivates me, sets me in motion. You are the force that turns stillness to motion. We come together until motion becomes stillness. This is our dance.

We came here to dance. We chose to come here because this is a place where they have dancing, why are we sitting at the bar? We chose to come here to experience being human. Let's take advantage of the situation, this night won't last forever.

### APRIL 29

"Use the shadow," I told her, "Write as though each day might be your last."

## April 30

Now the boat is almost a third of the way across the great ocean.

# *Chapter Five*

# MAY

## MAY 1

My power only feels like it's mine when I'm using it in service to something greater than me. And the truth is, I can often be in touch with that "something" without knowing or being able to put in words what it is. It's also true that I can *think* I know what it is, and yet *not* be in touch with it. So I tend to be cautious about defining what I'm serving, I don't like to give it a name.

I know how easily I can confuse myself, and I want to stay out of trouble.

I mention this to explain why I feel nervous and because I want to be very cautious about what I'm about to say. What I have to say is ridiculously simple, and doesn't deserve all this build-up, but it is the sort of thing that could be misunderstood. Anyway, here goes:

The great work of our time is planetary healing. The planet is our collective being (the biosphere, life on Earth), and we contribute to the work by sending out healing energy to the people and things around us. This can be as specific as tilling the soil or laying on hands, or it can be as general as maintaining an open heart and a loving spirit. What is noticeable is that more and more of us are involved in the conscious practice of healing. We are to some extent, sometimes, aware of ourselves as small, individual parts of the quickening process that is waking up our collective being, awakening the life force hidden in the egg preparing itself to be born.

Perhaps this image is too grandiose. All I'm trying to say is that we can't stay in our present situation, so we must allow ourselves to be transformed into what comes next. The *I Ching* describes this as revolution, or molting: the shedding of skin. Teilhard de Chardin is one of many modern thinkers who has presented a vision of humanity becoming something greater than it has been, a collective being with the moral and practical ability to play a greater role in the universe. If you like grand and glorious visions, this certainly lends itself to much romanticizing; if you prefer a more modest image of awakening, it would be easy to argue that the most outrageous and dramatic parts of our transformation are already behind us. The flavor and character of this change is highly subjective, which means that while it has a reality of its own, we can to a large extent choose our experience of it. The difference between sudden transformation and slow, steady growth lies very much in the eye of the beholder . . . you might say it depends on whether you're watching the outside or the inside of the cocoon.

I wrote an essay last year, and rewrote it, and rewrote it, and when it was finally done it was published as a pamphlet, under the name *Common Sense*. I'm going to try an experiment now; it fits the format and subject matter and style of this present book, I think, and I know it says what I want to say right now—so let's see what happens if I include it here as sections two through twenty-eight of chapter five.

Right now, if I had to say what it is I'm in service to, that's bigger than me, I'd call it the process of planetary healing. But I also know that, as big as that concept is, it may not be big enough. Perhaps no concept is ever big enough. Words and thoughts have their limitations. All we can do is follow our hearts.

### MAY 2

Our purpose here is to take action and have an effect on the world.

### MAY 3

We have been born into a moment of unprecedented danger and opportunity.
Our failure to act is itself a choice.
There is nowhere to hide from this awareness.

### MAY 4

It is time.

### MAY 5

It is time for each one of us to commit our energy, time, money, attention, to a vision of enduring peace and abundance—to a vision of humanity as a sound mind in the healthy body of the biosphere—to a vision of a world that works.
. . . to a vision of our children's children growing up in a world without war, a world committed to the freedom and dignity of every individual, regardless of race, sex, belief, or nation, a world committed to clean air, clean food, clean water for all . . . a world united in the awareness that in diversity lies strength . . . a world more full of love than hatred.

## MAY 6

It is time for each of us to vote with our lives—our daily lives—for or against the vision of a more hopeful future.

## MAY 7

Our purpose here is to build a bridge.

The purpose of the bridge is to span the distance between our present situation and our vision of a better world.

The beauty of a bridge is that, once it is in place, anyone can walk on it.

A few people can build a bridge that can be walked on by many.

## MAY 8

This is our response to the dangers that face us: we will build a bridge of faith over the great ocean.

## MAY 9

Every individual on earth is welcome to take part in this work.

It is as individuals, working alone or in groups, that we will accomplish our goals.

This is the greatest challenge we have ever faced. We humans are being given the opportunity to use what we've learned.

Hey, I see you, hiding under the rug there. Come out, my friend, and be of service. It's time.

## MAY 10

Breathe in, breathe out. Breathe in hope, breathe out fear. Breathe in courage, breathe out despair. The time for action has arrived.

Breathe in love, breathe out fatigue. Breathe in, breathe out. Fear keeps going out. There's never an end to it, but it's not a problem.

There are no problems.

Keep breathing.

## MAY 11

I am bringing forth my own energy. I can feel it welling up in me and pouring out into my work. I can't say thank you for the gifts fast enough. I can't stop crying out for more.

What a wonderful moment to be alive in!

## MAY 12

The momentum achieved by many different people in different places working towards a common goal is a tremendous source of encouragement and strength.

It allows each of us to approach our individual efforts with joy and energy and love.

And yet that moment always returns when we are alone with our uncertainties.

## MAY 13

On the edge of the dream we face our deepest doubts.

Now that it all is almost real, a terrible fear of success takes hold, and we grab desperately, uncontrollably, for failure.

One last chance to get off easy.

## MAY 14

Who among us really wants to save the world, to be born again into two thousand more years of struggle?

How much sweeter to be the doomed generation, float-ing gently on the errors and villainy of others, towards some glorious apocalypse now . . .

Hallelujah!, it's not my fault. Bring on the end times!

## MAY 15

We hate our enemies to provide ourselves in advance with excuses for possible failure.

Only when we give up the comforts of pessimism, the luxury of enemies, the sweetness of helplessness, can we see beyond our own doubts.

## MAY 16

I am speaking today of a great possibility, a chance to return to life, a chance to create a world for our children not worse than the one we have.

How dare I be discouraged in the work by anything so trivial as the fear of personal failure?

## MAY 17

Fear of success and fear of failure must be pushed aside and replaced with enthusiasm for the work at hand; every day a new beginning; let's go!

## MAY 18

There are bridges to build, new maps of consciousness to be delivered to every planetary address in every planetary language.

We are ironworkers, skywalkers, stubborn messengers of light and life.

## MAY 19

Oh friends, don't forget why we're here!

The truth is, we have the skills and we have the courage, if we could only keep our minds on what we really want.

When you know what you want, all things are possible.

## MAY 20

We want many things. Now is the time to take a look at our priorities. I can't believe we want security and comfort for ourselves *more* than we want good health and full lives for our children.

But our actions don't always express our priorities. Not because we don't care. Maybe because we're afraid to admit that our daily choices of where to commit our energies will make the difference.

We are afraid to admit that we could be building bridges right now.

## MAY 21

The truth is, we have everything to gain, and nothing to lose. The satisfaction of knowing you are doing your heart's work cannot be matched by any other pleasure on earth. The freedom of total service to a greater good is exactly what every seeker is searching for.

Maybe what really scares us is that if we stopped procrastinating, something real might happen.

## MAY 22

What is the nature of the work? I think the first step is to add yourself to the vision. Imagine that you have a specific role to play . . . and don't take no for an answer.

## MAY 23

Breathe in, breathe out.

It is time to remember what I already know. It is time to gather the tools I already have, time to walk forward naked in the direction where my heart's voice tells me to go, confident that my tools and my knowledge will be at hand when I need them.

Breathe in, breathe out. Fill my lungs with patience. Exhale anxiety and greed.

## MAY 24

Today I take a vow, not to love the world more than myself; not to love myself more than I love the world.

I vow to build a bridge over this gulf of imagination that pretends to separate my awareness of my own needs from my awareness of the needs of the planet.

We are one.

That means I must serve you, if I wish to please myself.

## MAY 25

Let us serve as models.

## MAY 26

And let us vow to enjoy our work so much that the hesitant and the fearful will grow jealous, and drop their chains, and run to join the fun.

## MAY 27

How to Prevent Nuclear War:
1. Admit that it could happen.
2. Decide that it will not happen.

3. Commit your vision and energy to number two without ever forgetting number one.

## MAY 28

To choose to build a bridge is the essential act of love.

## MAY 29

And now I've typed an entire book (pamphlet) that took me a year to write, and it's still the same afternoon. I even had time to go and pick up my car from the garage, where it was getting a new (rebuilt) alternator. And now *Common Sense* has been swallowed by *Waking Up Together.* But it's all right. I saw Jorge Luis Borges speak in New York in 1968, he said that as a writer grows older he endeavors to say the same thing in fewer and fewer words. Ultimately he would get it down to a few pages, a page, a paragraph, a sentence, a word. Borges didn't say so (or I didn't hear him), but if one should live so long one might find that people are uncomfortable reading a mere word or paragraph, so the writer might go on to hide his word or paragraph in a larger body of prose created for the purpose, like one powerful modest man in a congress of politicians, or a bit of DNA hidden in a mountainous molecule of inert matter.

Of course I don't mean to say that this book is a mountain of inert matter, but if it were that would be just fine as long as it served its purpose. And what is that purpose? I don't know. I want to help people be in touch with their own power. I want to encourage the healers to love themselves and keep themselves healthy, so that your touch (for you are a healer, every person who reads this) will be of real value and will play its part in the collective creation of a new world (new point of view, new attitude) that I call waking up together.

And my purpose also is to please myself. There's no altruism here. I don't love you because I'm a nice guy, I love you for the pleasure I find in your beautiful face.

77

## MAY 30

And I'm left with the question, how does healing awaken?

## MAY 31

What comes to mind is the myth of the kiss that awakens the sleeping princess. I believe we (the people of this planet) already are that powerful being we aspire to. And fear of our power, of the responsibility, all that, has encouraged us to make ourselves sick, to cloud our minds and hearts, to delay us from taking the next giant step. The payoff for being sick is, you get to hang out in a state of "I'm not ready." There's something I really should be thinking about, but it'll have to wait till I'm feeling better.

And the healer's touch removes not the sickness but the fear itself, it removes the need for the sickness. At that point, the sickness becomes a purging, a cleansing, a release, we can surrender to it and go with it for however long it takes and wake up renewed and refreshed and discover that we've already taken the giant step. And here we are on the other side.

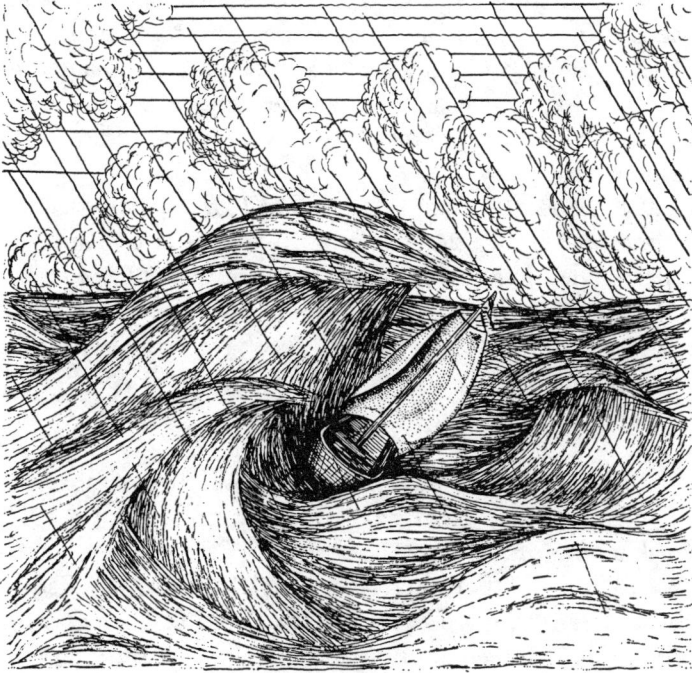

# Chapter Six

# JUNE

**JUNE 1**

While I've been writing this book, a guy named Bird has been rowing a boat across the Pacific Ocean. I haven't followed his adventures closely, but I have seen much mention of them in the local paper because Bird's financial backer lives in the small town I live near. Anyway, this morning's paper has headlines saying he's run into terrible storms less than 25 miles from his destination in Australia. He has asked to be rescued—what a surrender, to be willing to give in and accept fate after crossing that whole ocean and coming so close to victory!—but they can't find him (his local sponsor is among those out on boats in the Australia storms searching for him). As I write this, Bird may be dead, he may be rescued, or he may even have successfully reached shore and become the first known modern person to row alone across our largest ocean. What a story!

My life is also such a story, and I firmly believe yours is, whether you recognize it or not. Are you not caught up in a great struggle of the heart? No? Are you sure? Look again . . .

Suddenly I think of one of my favorite pieces of writing. Since it is not in copyright, and you have probably read it no more recently than I, if at all, I'll share it with you here:

### The Lee Shore

Some chapters back, one Bulkington was spoken of, a tall, new-landed mariner, encountered in New Bedford at the inn.

When on that shivering winter's night, the Pequod thrust her vindictive bows into the cold malicious waves, who should I see standing at her helm but Bulkington! I looked with sympathetic awe and fearfulness upon the man, who in mid-winter just landed from a four years' dangerous voyage, could so unrestingly push off again for still another tempestuous term. The land seemed scorching to his feet. Wonderfullest things are ever the unmentionable; deep memories yield no epitaphs; this six-inch chapter is the stoneless grave of Bulkington. Let me only say that it fared with him as with the storm-tossed ship, that miserably drives along the leeward land. The port would fain give succor; the port is pitiful; in the port is safety, comfort, hearthstone, supper, warm blankets, friends, all that's kind to our mortalities! But in that gale, the port, the land, is that ship's direst jeopardy; she must fly all hospitality; one touch of land, though it but graze the keel, would make her shudder through and through. With all her might she crowds all sail off shore; in so doing, fights 'gainst the very winds that fain would blow her homeward; seeks all the lashed sea's landlessness again; for refuge's sake forlornly rushing into peril; her only friend her bitterest foe!

Know ye, now, Bulkington? Glimpses do ye seem to see of that mortally intolerable truth; that all deep, earnest thinking is but the intrepid effort of the soul to keep the open independence of her sea; while the wildest winds of heaven and earth conspire to cast her on the treacherous, slavish shore?

But as in landlessness alone resides the highest truth, shoreless, indefinite as God—so, better is it to perish in that howling infinite, than be ingloriously dashed upon the lee, even if that were safety! For worm-like, then, oh! who would craven crawl to land! Terrors of the terrible! is all this agony so vain? Take heart, take heart, O Bulkington! Bear thee grimly, demigod! Up from the spray of thy ocean-perishing—straight up, leaps thy apotheosis!

—Herman Melville, *Moby Dick,* chapter 23

I wish Mr. Bird well this evening. I want to make it clear that I admire his surrender, his willingness to call for help, as much as any other aspect of his intrepid undertaking; and his uncertain fate even now reminds me that all we can ever truly do is surrender to the will of God, which Bird surely did the moment he began his crossing. Human nobility and glory lie not in our willingness to challenge God, as Ahab imagined, but in our willingness to undertake the crossing though we know full well we have no ultimate control. California to Australia or Earth to Moon, I pray and believe the symbol of our era will be the crossing and not the cross.

## JUNE 2

The dictionary definition of "apotheosis" is, "the act of raising a person to the status of a god." And the other news this evening is that in just a few hours a spaceship from Earth, Pioneer 10, will be leaving the solar system, the first ever to do so, a human artifact (still alive, still sending back information) crossing the orbit of the furthest-known planet and heading out towards infinity. Goodbye. Hello.

## June 3

How can you be alive and aware in 1983 and *not* be a romantic?, I wonder.

## June 4

What constantly amazes me about the subject of men and women is that it's so important in my life. I have never really been able to give my mind a satisfactory explanation for this. What is desire? The notion I keep coming back to is that desire is the form in which we experience the essential restlessness of the universe. Attraction/repulsion. "If you gotta go," says Bob Dylan, "well, it's all right. But if you gotta go, go now, or else you gotta stay all night."

Another notion I just can't shake is that sexual desire and the desire for knowledge, desire for fame, desire for money, desire for peace of mind or spiritual understanding, are all a lot closer to being the same experience than we ordinarily realize. And of these, sexual desire is the most elegant, the most complex, the most immediate, most mysterious, the one that reveals the most about our human condition, the one that succeeds in reminding us how little we really know about ourselves.

What do I want? I want what I think I can have, or maybe just a little bit more than that (to make life interesting). Well fine. And so here's how to throw me or any other person into total confusion: present me with what seems to be a very real possibility of having a whole lot more of something I want, let me suddenly think I can have a whole lot more than I usually think possible. Tilt! You have to do this with a certain finesse, of course, so you engage my vanity instead of just throwing me into terror. Terror is easy to deal with: I shut down. Vanity, on the other hand, is a real challenge, especially to those of us who pretend or believe we're not into that. It's real easy to hook someone when you grab onto a part of them that they're pretending isn't there.

There is a puritanical reaction to this information I'm presenting, which is to say categorically that temptation is

82

Bad, desire is Bad, and the only way to save your ass is to stay the hell away from all this stuff. Never let yourself be tempted! Uh huh. Good luck.

And there's an inverse to this rule that we want what we think we can have, plus a little more. The inverse is, the less you think you can have, or the less you allow yourself to have, the more opportunities there are for severe temptation. People who willfully deprive themselves experience far more temptation in their lives than other folks. Everything's a temptation! And so by rejecting temptation you get to experience it five times as much.

There's all kinds of desire, as I said before, but I like sex because it's both the simplest and the most complex. An attractive person of the opposite sex (or whatever you're attracted to) can come along and look at you a certain way (thus suggesting that what you believe isn't possible might be possible) and throw all your theories and beliefs out the window. There are all sorts of defenses, of course, like making yourself unattractive, and they all involve various degrees of shutting down. But what fascinates me right now is the flip side of this, the way it can be used as an opportunity to open up. I'm not at all sure how open I'm willing to get, but letting myself experience and respond to desire is an interesting way to find out!

### JUNE 5

When I talk about the essential restlessness of the universe, I'm referring to Brownian movement, which my dictionary describes as "the constant, random, zigzag movement of small particles dispersed in a fluid medium." (I do notice there's been a lot of zigzagging in my life lately, with desire often the apparent motivator and seemingly random movement the observable result.)

I have always had a fondness for Brownian movement. Here's what I heard when it was first described to me, back in high school: that when we get down to the smallest things we can perceive, we discover that they're all in motion and that those motions cannot be predicted or explained. (They can be predicted statistically, but not individually.) In other words, the basic character of the universe is not stillness but motion, not order but "disorder."

I put the word disorder in quotes because it is an expression of human vanity: the underlying assumption here is that "order" is that which humans can explain, predict, understand. I disagree; I happen to love the idea that there is an order to things that defies our understanding, and always will (we get closer, we get further away). I guess I'm a religious nut. I love science, because it explores and illuminates the unknown. But I think those who think the purpose of science is to destroy and eliminate the unknown (and the sooner the better) are really out of their minds.

## JUNE 6

The desire for security is usually what drives us out of our minds.

## JUNE 7

Dear J——,
There are and have been many "J"s in my life; you know who you are but the reader doesn't, so I need to say that you are not my friend in Switzerland, you are another, equally powerful creature walking around on Earth disguised as a beautiful woman. Or is it a disguise? Oh yes, now I remember, we are what we appear to be. You know, I have a stubborn belief that my attraction to beauty is some kind of foolishness. I mean, it bothers me that I would give you less attention if your face, body, hands were not so physically attractive to my eyes. And now I'm thinking, if we are what we appear to be, then this prejudice of mine could actually be wisdom.

Yesterday I was with a friend, a lover, who I am not strongly attracted to. I like making love with her, it's comfortable and satisfying and she appreciates me. And yet I can be bored in her presence, and that's not good—it makes me irritable, unpleasant to myself and to her. It feels like she and I have had a great healing impact on each other, and now it's time to go on. Maybe that means, move our relationship out of the sexual realm. My fear or my belief is, however, that then I wouldn't bother to spend time with her at all. In which case I'd feel guilty. But that might mean I'm starting to be with her from a sense of obligation, and I don't like that. What a trap. I even worry about how she'll feel if and when she reads these words. Which means I'm afraid to tell her how I feel. See how I create these things for myself?

And then last night I was with you, and I notice how we didn't make love. And according to the rule, that means I didn't want to.

I am attracted to and afraid of your power. I hang out with less powerful (less attractive) people because it's safe. Oh, my other friend is attractive enough—she'd have men beating down her door if she wanted that—but this is not about how things "really are," this is about how they look to me. I look at you and feel lust. I reach for you and keep you at a distance at the same time. You do the same to me. Fear/desire. I like to pretend that I want you more than you want me. It's not really true. But I wonder why I like to pretend that?

Still talking to myself. What will it take for me to be able to talk to you?

Thank you for your patience with me.

Love,
Paul

## JUNE 8

And the late news is that Peter Bird did get rescued, off the Great Barrier Reef, five minutes before the breaking up of his boat and certain death. And in this way completed his crossing, not as he had pictured it perhaps but with the dignity and satisfaction of a person who has done his possible— every inch of the possible—and lived to tell the tale.

## JUNE 9

I'm on the beach at Santa Monica with my two sons, it's early evening of the longest day of the year. My neck is sore, maybe partly from carrying a shoulder bag around all day yesterday at Disneyland, and from sleeping uncomfortably on a strange bed (sofa) last night. But mostly, I believe, my neck is sore because I'm feeling wounded and vulnerable. This same muscle has ached for the same apparent reason a number of times in the last eight months, and I may as well admit that I know what it means. When I deny or ignore my body's messages, I only succeed in forcing it to speak louder.

Attraction/repulsion is driving me crazy. Where does the desire for security fit into this? I guess I want to feel *sure* that I want her and that she wants me, or else that we really can't stand each other, and not have it flip back and forth the way it does. Today my friend told me he told his girlfriend they weren't sexually compatible, and she said, "So what?" He acknowledges that this was an impressive display of her power.

Today I'm very aware that I lack the ability to be detached about my sexual fears and desires. What do I want? Well, I'd like to have a beautiful woman in my bed tonight. And I'd also like her to be kind to me. Sometimes I think I want too much.

There's a woman up north somewhere very angry at me today (I imagine) because I told her no when she asked to spend the solstice with me. And another woman to the south I'm angry at, because she said no to me. And so it goes, on and on. And I know we do it to ourselves. I wounded myself, and used her as an instrument. It ain't much fun for her, I suppose. And not much fun for me.

And my desire for security makes me want to go home and get under the covers and promise myself that I won't mess with no outrageous beauties, no more. I don't like being vulnerable. I don't like to practice what I preach, about living in the moment. I don't like making a fool of myself. I guess I must be human.


## JUNE 10

I guess the point is that you and I are also rowing our boats, alone, across the great ocean. Our whole objective is to reach land, security, and yet we clearly chose to leave the land and abandon security when we decided to set out on this voyage. And maybe I'm wrong to say our objective is to reach land, to come through this safely. It would be more accurate to say that our objective is to make the crossing. And if we were other than naked and alone, the crossing would lose its meaning.

We have chosen to experience the limitations of being human. I don't think of us as sinners. I think of us all as avatars, pieces of Christ or Krishna, rising like yeast and un-avoidably raising the entire loaf of life-on-Earth with us as we rise.

### JUNE 11

Life is funny. Our publishing business got a letter this morning from an old distributor, recapitulating our account and saying we owe them $600. I opened it and thought, hmph, maybe we do—it didn't sound right but I don't know, better check it out, anyway we're in no position to pay them. I pulled the file and found that their figures were accurate except they'd forgotten two outstanding invoices, and actually *they* owe *us* $800. I'll copy the invoices and write them a letter; and probably they'll send back a big shipment of books they haven't sold, to make up the balance (I know they still have a lot of human rights books in their warehouse). So it's no big deal; just kind of funny how it turns around.

This chapter has been partly concerned with the question of desire, and my dismay at how little control I have over my sexual desire at times. And the last few days have provided turnaround as the universe and a couple of delight-ful women have allowed me to experience being the object of strong desire. I like it! I like being able to let myself be as gentle and powerful as I really am.

So today I feel real good about being open and vulner-able. Tomorrow it may turn around again, and that's all right too. Open means open to joy *and* pain. I don't have to pre-tend that the pain is joy to convince myself to stay open. I can let the pain be pain, and suffer through it, and choose to stay open anyway.

And if I close up for a while, it's no great disaster. It's a bit of a trap: a body at rest tends to stay at rest, and we all know we're capable of staying closed and stuck for years at a time, once we get into it. No fun. But no great disaster, I say, because the truth is no matter what I think in my mind, at any given moment I can choose to be open and to feel my feelings again. When I'm awake, it really doesn't matter how long I slept. What matters is what's happening right now.


## JUNE 12

Life is funny. Maybe the fact that we think of "awakening" as a big dramatic event is sometimes the biggest barrier to being awake. Instead of quietly opening our eyes and our hearts, we sit here waiting for something big to happen.


## JUNE 13

Obviously it isn't helpful if we say "it's all right to close up" and then use that as an excuse to run and hide every time things get the least bit challenging. ("Challenging" = interesting, difficulty means opportunity. If we avoid challenges and difficult stuff, life gets boring and there never seem to be any opportunities to improve matters. To read these words with a sense of smugness, like it applies to other people but not to me, is real foolishness. If you believe there's nothing in your life that you're avoiding, then you are asleep indeed.)

And at the same time it's really not helpful to say "it's not all right to close up," because that inevitably leads to the idea that we have something to lose, it makes us very tight and rigid as we try to hold on to this state of being awake and open.

We have nothing to lose. The only thing we need to carry around with us is the awareness that no matter how far gone we are, at any given moment we can choose to open our hearts and our eyes, and be here.

## JUNE 14

"But I don't know *how* to be open!" It's simple enough. Just acknowledge your feelings, let yourself feel what you really feel, without censorship or judgment. If you don't know what you're feeling, acknowledge that you don't know what you're feeling. And if there's another person in your sphere of vision, choose to have the courage (pretend to have the courage) to share your feelings with that person. Take a risk. Don't be aggressive, don't try to protect yourself. Just let down the barriers and tell them what you feel.

## JUNE 15

"I don't understand *why* this is so difficult for me." Beware of the trap of the "why" question. Don't try to find out "why?". It doesn't help. What helps is taking action. Open yourself, with no expectations. See what happens.

## JUNE 16

If you're not satisfied with the results, that's perfect. Look at your dissatisfaction. Now you know what your expectations were.

Now open yourself, with no expectations. See what happens.

## JUNE 17

My mind is a blank. I feel like I've been sitting here for weeks, waiting to see what words will come out of my typewriter. It's interesting. Writing is a naked process, it brings you up against your demons. On the surface of things, I feel fine. Everything's all right, things are moving right along. But as I sit here, some mysterious voice inside me says things aren't what they seem. I feel fear. And it's about this book I'm writing, or else it's about what the book is about: being in the moment, allowing myself to be who I am. The file folder in which I carry around the pages I've already written is getting thick. On the surface of things, that's terrific. I've written a lot, and I like what I've written. And I know I have a lot more to say. I should be happy. But I'm scared. I don't really understand it, but experience (not reason) tells me it must be about fear of my power. Suddenly I remember a story my mother tells about my fifth birthday. She found me upstairs in my room, sobbing uncontrollably. "What's wrong?" This question had to be asked quite a number of times, in different ways, before I finally blurted out my answer: "I don't want to be five! I want to be the same old four I always was!"

I love growth, but I hate getting bigger. Isn't there some way I can have the sensation of moving forward without actually leaving this place where everything's so familiar and comfortable?

### June 18

Q: But didn't you say you can't stand things the way they are?

A: Yes, but if they get any better, how do I know I'll be able to handle it?

### June 19

One aspect of this hesitation I'm feeling, this fear of my power, has to do with my willingness to share myself with you. I don't feel very giving right now. I do this a lot, actually. People ask me questions, and I frown in a way that makes them wish they hadn't asked.

Maybe it's good that I'm forcing myself to write to you in spite of this reluctance I feel. If I only wrote to you at those moments when I'm willing to share myself, you'd get a distorted picture of who I am.

"Look at how open this guy is!" "Yeah, that's because he'll never let you see him when he's closed."

I'm not suggesting I "should" be open all the time. But

there's a difference between closing up because it's time to rest, and closing up because things are starting to happen. What bothers me is that now that my work is really starting to go places, some part of me wants to run as fast as it can in the other direction.

## JUNE 20

What's happening in my life lately is I've been letting go of my pictures of "how it's supposed to be," replacing those pictures with new temporary pictures, and now I seem to be gripped with insecurity as I notice I'm not able to hang on even to the new temporary replacement pictures. My wife was going to move out of our house at the end of the month, and get her own place, and now that's unclear. I continue to have no idea where I am financially, and whether I should tell the printer to reprint the books that are almost out of stock. The latter question confused me so much that I finally came to the realization that I didn't have to decide. But now I'm making myself nervous about it again. Probably the business with my wife is the big thing: lots of uncertainty, about money, whether she's around or not and whether I can handle it or not, questions about childcare, communication . . . I keep saying it's not bad, most separations are a lot messier, more hostile, and that's true but it doesn't change the fact that the situation is a real challenge to me. What did I say a few pages back? Challenges make life interesting. Okay. Difficult situations are actually opportunities. Yeah, I can believe it. So what can I do? Give myself the space to be insecure, make dinner for the boys, take care of what's in front of me day to day, and don't forget to make some time to be with myself.

I had been considering joining the nonviolent blockade of the Livermore nuclear weapons laboratory ten days ago, I felt willing to go to jail for a few days to make a statement about the importance of ending our personal and national involvement in such research. Well, I'm not sure how willing I was, but I was attracted by the possibility of being part of that activity, to know that I was really doing something and to experience the possible deepening of my own commitment as a result (that happened when I took part in a fast against the Vietnam War seventeen years ago). So I was attracted, I mentioned it to people, and the next step would have been to do the nonviolent training and get more information and see if I still felt ready. And then my wife said that she had a lot of commitments that week regarding her music, and it wouldn't work for her to be stuck with childcare if I ended up in jail. And that along with other scheduling problems prodded me to let go of the idea. Maybe my fear of going to jail was also a factor in dropping the idea. I'm sure it was, although resistance to that fear was also one of the factors making me want to go through with it, once the idea entered my head. So I was kind of pushing myself in both directions.

Anyway now ten days later most of the blockaders (there were close to a thousand) are still in jail, and may be facing $500 fines. I'm pretty sure I wouldn't have taken part, at this time in my life, if I'd known the stakes might be so heavy. And, well, the whole situation stirs up some questions for me that I can't answer easily. I know that I'm contributing to "the solution" by my writing, my teaching, even my personal impact on folks I meet and spend time with. And the best thing I can do, the only thing I can do, is be myself. I know this, and still I wonder if my actions live up to my words. Should I be doing more? That answers itself. I don't believe in "should"s.

You know what? I think what's really operating is my vanity. I want to "look like" I'm doing something. That's not the same as doing something, and it can be dangerous, especially if we don't know what's motivating us. Okay. The next thing to do is take a walk and just explore what I'm doing with my time and energy these days—I'm probably doing fine, but it would be wise to explore the question, since it's come up, rather than just try to bury it with an automatic response. ("I'm doing great. Shut up already.")

Letting go of pictures, old pictures, new pictures. I feel like I'm falling through space, endlessly, Alice down the rabbit hole. And actually quite a lot of the time I do relax and let myself enjoy it. But I also get nervous and confused and scared and uncertain. It comes with the territory, and I'm slowly outgrowing the illusion that I need to *do* something about it. It's okay to feel what I feel. Maybe I should keep telling myself that until I believe it. "Should." Oh Lord. I'll go make dinner now.

## JUNE 21

It's as though there's something more I need to say before I can allow myself to go to bed. Something is driving me. My younger son asked me today, why does Mom have to live somewhere else? I talked with him about it, but I noticed it was very difficult for me to say anything. I don't know the answer. I told him we don't want to live with each other now. A generation ago my father told me something similar when I asked why he had left us. These questions are difficult for everyone. And the truth is, I want to open up more. I want to be more able to say what I'm feeling, not just on paper but face to face and heart to heart. And slowly but surely I'm getting what I want. And choking on it at times. And still asking for more.

## JUNE 22

Thank you, God, for these gifts of pain and confusion and surrender. And love.

## JUNE 23

Women and men
move back and forth
In between
effect and cause;
Just beyond the range of normal sight
This glittering joker
was dancing in the dragon's jaws.
—Bruce Cockburn

93

I am writing to you tonight from as sure a manifestation of the midnight hour as I have experienced or can imagine. This is a party that I have been at, on and off, for twenty years. Literally, the same party, with many of the same people, in different hotel rooms in different cities at different times. The party never seems to end; just gets adjourned till the next installment, which by the way is never announced, and can only be recognized as a genuine installment after one has been at it for hours. (Although in another sense you recognize it the moment you walk in the door. And realize you have been vaguely searching, or maybe just waiting, since the last time.)

### June 24

It is quite likely that you will never attend an installment of the particular party I refer to. Or you may. But it is certain that you have your own version of this party. When you look around and notice you're in the middle of it again, you are having an experience of the midnight hour.

### June 25

Now I am sitting in a hotel lobby at five o'clock in the morning. If you've ever been in a hotel lobby at five in the morning with no certain knowledge of what you're doing there, you know exactly how I feel.

And something I do like about this hotel is it has an endless expanse of lobby.

### June 26

This lobby that stretches on forever in all directions reminds me of the sand on the Oregon dunes.

This is what Kerouac referred to as "the golden eternity."

## JUNE 27

Zig. Zag. A primary theme of this book you're reading is, being in the moment. A secondary theme is the midnight hour, our personal experiences of timelessness. These themes are not the same: our minds might argue that being in the moment is the essence of timelessness, but our experience says otherwise.

That state of timelessness that we achieve at various odd and unpredictable moments in our lives certainly does not occur every time we allow ourselves to be in the moment, to feel what we're feeling and be here for what's happening right now (detached from considerations about the past or the future). Being in the moment does not lead to timelessness. Timelessness, on the other hand, does give us a taste of being in the moment in a powerful and almost mystical fashion: when you're in the midnight hour, you seem to be in a place where there is no possibility of being distracted and falling out of the moment. There's nowhere else to go. Outside of time there is no past and future; you can relax; you can't help but relax; you are free.

Timelessness comes to us as a gift. Being in the moment is sometimes a gift, sometimes a discipline (something we practice). We do it both consciously and unconsciously. We can choose at any moment to let go of our considerations and notice here and now. By practicing this, we use our experience of (contact with) the golden eternity to aid us in our daily lives. But to feel suffused with the golden eternity is not something we can arrive at by will, by choice. We can open our sails to the winds of eternity, but we cannot force them to blow. Even patience is no guarantee. There is no specific door to the midnight hour.

## JUNE 28

And to try to hold on to those golden moments is a formula for endless, sweet sadness (after a while probably more bitter than sweet). Kerouac tells us this with his writings and his life. If you want to read a beautiful fable on the subject, check out "The Piper at the Gates of Dawn," chapter seven of *The Wind in the Willows*. "Piper" says we must forget the music, or live always in pain of its absence. This is true. The God Pan is kind to Mole and Water Rat, and gives them forgetfulness.

As we aspire to higher consciousness, as we move (as we force ourselves to move, for example with nuclear weapons) from being God's creatures to being as Gods, as we discover that we have choice, we find that forgetfulness is not enough. To choose to be conscious is to choose not to forget.

So we live always in pain. And every day, every moment, we must let go of this pain. To let go means to stop holding on to what we don't have. (I lost an important notebook yesterday; I'm having a hell of a time letting go of it.)

If we won't let go of our pain (fear, doubt, desire), day to day and moment to moment, survival causes us to be overcome with forgetfulness in spite of ourselves. The very act of holding on becomes a form of forgetting. We go unconscious. We fall asleep, pass out.

To stay awake, we need a conscious act of release. We can't hold on to those magic moments; we can't hold on to all the things we've done wrong. We need to remember them but not be attached to them. To stay conscious, we must practice techniques for letting go of our pain at every moment.

### June 29

Letting go is like breathing. It solves no problems, gets rid of nothing. You take one breath, you have to take another. Letting go of our pain doesn't get rid of it. It allows it to be there, and then we have to let go of it again. Crazy, isn't it? But it works.

### June 30

The opposite of letting go is holding on. Hold your

breath as long as you can. Even with the greatest will power in the world, the best you can do is force yourself into unconsciousness.

Go ahead, tiger, knock yourself out. See where it gets you.

# Chapter Seven

# JULY

**JULY 1**

If I reach as far into myself as I possibly can, perhaps I will find something that I am willing to share or give. It seems strange to me, that I should be so eager to open myself at one moment, and so recalcitrant the next. I am really reluctant to let anyone see into my heart. I want to curl up into a ball, and roll through these next few days completely self-contained.

And on the other hand that's not what I want at all. I am impatient with this withdrawal of mine, if it's necessary I'm willing to go along with it but I'd really rather break through it and suddenly discover or create a whole new vein of energy and love and enthusiasm. I want to have some fun, and I want to be fun to be around.

It's coming. My heart turns towards the light, turns away again, returns. I don't know where I'm going but I'm ready to go. Hello universe. Something's happening here.

## JULY 2

Courage is not always romantic. Often it's the tiniest thing. For example: it takes courage to say you're afraid, instead of just keeping your mouth shut and forcing the other person to decide for herself what's going on. Maybe sometimes it takes courage to wash the dishes or file some papers when you're up against an inner obstacle, instead of playing solitaire or reading a magazine . . . because in choosing to do a small, order-creating task you are really choosing to put yourself in a position where you'll be able and willing to attack the problem, you're moving towards action and response rather than ducking the issue altogether. That would be courage, choosing to take a small but real step instead of sitting in confusion and refusing to choose.

Another time, of course, washing the dishes or cleaning your desk or even something ambitious like rototilling the garden could be a total avoidance, a way of getting away from (pretending to get away from) what's bothering you when in fact the most courageous thing would be to sit quietly with your difficulty and do nothing and allow yourself to admit its reality.

It all depends on the situation. My point is that courage can express itself in ways that are small and subtle and not at all what we expect. Sometimes it takes a lot of courage to be willing to look like a coward. We all live in terror of other people's judgments. And it often happens that willingness to face that fear and not be controlled by it is the only path to freedom.

## JULY 3

In the early chapters of this book I mentioned several times a woman named Judith, who won my heart when I visited Switzerland last fall. We exchanged a lot of letters after I got back to America (and tapes and gifts and phone calls) and made plans to work together and be together again in early spring, plans that fell apart because the intensity of our relationship made us both crazy . . . each of us became more crazy than the other, in his or her crazy state, could handle. I flipped into obsession/possession (adoration), and she simultaneously (although you could say her action triggered mine, or mine triggered hers) turned turtle and pulled into her shell and shouted, "No!"

And there we left it, a Mexican standoff (guns at each other's heads), followed by cautious, deliberate, simultaneous withdrawal and a sort of a helpless, respectful silence, both maybe hoping that the next time we meet, if there is one, we won't have to reenact the same movie but can start again with a different script or none at all. And even our disengagement, for all its anger and bitterness, had moments of the same raw power and extraordinary grace and mutual awakening that had characterized our connection from the beginning.

I mention it now only because I notice I've been terrified to say anything about it (a terror disguised as polite reluctance, uncertainty). I guess I've been going on the assumption that the wound is healed and have been scared to find out whether that's true or not. Which means it's not healed, long as I'm ruled by that fear.

But it's a real good sign that I've written this section. This is my way of taking my own advice, this is my small but real step, my tiny flag of courage in the face of my doubts and fears. I learned so much from that woman! And now I have to live with not knowing how we feel about each other.

## JULY 4

In fact, "not knowing" is probably what I have to learn to live with in all my relationships. It sure ain't easy.

Awakening is painful, and part of the pain I'm feeling now is that I'm having difficulty believing my own ideas. I have said in this writing that person-to-person healing is the form in which planetary healing is expressed and accomplished. I believe this; it is consistent with my vision and my experience. And the words, when I say them or read them, have for me the unmistakable ring of truth. And yet at the same time I notice that I am having difficulty accepting this concept in practice.

What bothers me is that this book (and my life, which this book reflects) seems far more concerned with private issues (relationships, doubts and fears, desire, courage, self-awareness) than public ones (planetary awakening, human rights, reversing the drift towards nuclear holocaust). I feel as though I am indulging myself. I know I'd much rather go out and fall in love with yet another pretty face than march on a protest line. I tell myself that marching on a protest line is as much an expression of private drives as any other activity, but I'm not convinced. I still feel there's an imbalance. I feel I'm talking the talk but not walking the walk: I'm not taking action for what I believe in. And my book is full of private advice instead of collective vision.

See what I mean? If I truly believe that person-to-person healing is the form in which planetary healing is accomplished, why do I have these anxieties? I know that keeping ourselves healthy (grounded, in touch with the moment) is the most important factor in effectively healing others. And I know that what I'm writing and what I'm doing in my life is of real practical value for the people I come in contact with. I'm giving what I can give, now more than ever. And yet there's this voice in me that puts me down, that says I'm missing the boat.

Private vs. public. It's a phony distinction. "I vow to build a bridge over this gulf of imagination that pretends to separate my awareness of my own needs from my awareness of the needs of the planet." Divide and conquer. The voice that says, "Williams, you're getting too personal, you're ignoring the needs of the planet," is the force that separates. Guilt and self-doubt are its weapons.

And yet even as I say this, I see how the pendulum can swing the other way, how I could use this notion of "the voice that separates" as a way of blocking self-examination and self-awareness . . . I could use it for self-justification. I could pretend that any inner voice that tries to wake me up is just trying to lead me astray.

Insight is a two-edged sword. Again, I caution both you and me: don't try to destroy your doubts. It is better to live with them. It is necessary to live with them. They're painful. But if we let ourselves be aware of them and don't get locked in combat with them, they won't interfere with our power.

So here I am writing about how to live with doubts. And, despite my doubts, I know that in doing so I'm making my contribution to the cause of planetary awakening.

### July 6

"Don't Doubt Yourself, Babe" is a song by Jackie DeShannon, recorded by the Byrds on their first album in 1965. I'd like to have it translated into the appropriate languages and play it for all the world's leaders, all four and a half billion of us.

### July 7

Saturday, it's about noon. I have a new job, literary executor for a writer who many consider to have been one of the great novelists of the twentieth century (in any language) . . . last night I was up till three reading one of his unpublished novels, very excited to find such a good one among the vast quantities of papers he left behind. Now I need to call my employer, the administrator of his estate, his oldest daughter. He and I were good friends, now it's kind of like a dump truck has come and dumped his whole life into my office, many thousands of pages of correspondence, novels that were considered unpublishable (that will all be published now) because they're outside the realm where he achieved his reputation during his lifetime, his thousands of sheets of theological/philosophical notes that could someday be of tremendous interest and importance, plus letters arriving here every day from his friends and fans around the world, whew, what have I got myself into? Actually, I had my eyes open on this one: I knew it would be big, complex, exciting, overwhelming, I could have said yes or no and I said yes with enthusiasm. I'm willing to give up being a publisher in order to do this work for the estate. I'm not willing to give up being a writer, and I don't have to. Just the usual juggling act.

Priorities. I was eager to get to the typewriter this morning. *Waking Up Together* has been sleeping in me for a few days, gestating, and now it's impatient to spill onto paper. But even though it would be easy to argue in the abstract that nothing I'm doing right now is more important than writing this book, in practice lots of things that may not seem more important on a cosmic scale do and must take precedence in the moment. Of course I went to get the mail. Otherwise I'd be sitting here impossibly distracted by the knowledge that the mail and its surprises are waiting for me, the only way for me to stop that is to surrender and see what's in the p.o. box today and get it out of my system. And then Taiyo and his friend who stayed over need breakfast (Kenta stayed over at someone else's house), and I pour a little cereal for myself too, and the boys had mentioned to me when I got up that they found more boards with nails sticking out of them in the backyard (they play with boards and two-by-fours a lot, sometimes they nail 'em together and then when they get pulled apart again nasty sharp rusted nails stick out to be stepped on, fallen on), so there's an absolute priority, almost absolute, I told 'em to be careful and I'd come and remove all the nails as soon as I got the mail and gave them some breakfast. The urge to write has to wait till I know I'm not risking having some youngster's foot punctured.

And I read one long letter from an old pal who has much to say, and talked briefly with my neighbor about the book I read last night, and now here I am ready to write, except I

would like to make that phone call first and then I'll be right
with you.


JULY 8

Another kind of priority is the emergency, earlier this
week we had something like seven emergency calls in two and
a half days, we being the small town volunteer fire department I've belonged to for the last seven years. People ask
how often I get called out on emergencies, it's impossible to
answer, we can go for weeks with no calls at all, and then they
all bunch up at once. I've been at some good-sized fires,
sometimes one after another, but we've also had a period of
years when we never had a fire worth mentioning (fine with
me, though of course we all get tired of automobile accidents,
of which there seem to be more all the time). Anyway this
past week we were having one of our summer heatwaves,
107° by mid-afternoon (but dry; it's bad, but maybe not as
monstrous as you'd imagine), and we had a series of grass
fires, vehicle accidents and medical aids that wouldn't quit.
Possible arson on some of the grass fires, although the worst
was clearly started by downed power lines, that was in mid-
afternoon of one of the hottest days and after scrambling up
a hill with hose in my hands and more in a pack on my back,
knocking down the flames on my flank of the fire and then
walking through the burn hitting hot spots, I found myself
with a great need to sit down and open my fire-retardant suit
and cool off and rest for a while. By this time our partners
from the state department of forestry (active in the summer
only) were doing most of the clean-up. The fire was controlled
very quickly; when you don't get quick control, it's really hard
to rest, sometimes impossible because too dangerous (but dangerous not to rest, also). The professionals with forestry have
to deal with that fairly often, I guess; I'm glad I'm just a small
town volunteer. It's not like I'm on call for any emergency,
anywhere; I respond only to emergencies in my particular
community. (And adjacent areas when something big happens
and they need our help.) Limits make service possible.

(I have to remember that about limits as I get into this work for the estate. I promised them 20% of my working time, and naturally I'll give somewhat more than that at the beginning, getting things underway, but I need to remember not to overdo it and burn myself out, that doesn't help anyone. And I need to remember that it's up to me to set my own limits, instead of just automatically responding to everything that comes my way, till it chokes me.)

The emergency call is a very high priority, but not quite absolute. If I were taking care of my neighbors' two-year-old when the fire radio (a one-way radio that turns itself on and shouts at us) went off, I wouldn't go until or unless I found someone else to be with her (when my kids were smaller I would sometimes take them to the station with me, if I were alone with them—I couldn't go to the emergency but I might be able to dispatch, freeing someone else to go).

It is useful, though, still talking about priorities, to have the repeated learning experience that almost anything, no matter how urgent it seems, can be interrupted by something more urgent. I'll be desperately trying to finish up some things so I can take off for an appointment I'm already late for, or to take care of something that urgently needs to get in the mail today, and then the fire radio goes off and all I can do is let go. Surrender to the moment, surrender to God's will, stop pretending (for a moment) that I'm in control of all this stuff.

And how bad can I feel about my missed deadline or screwed-up appointment, when confronted with a person whose neat plans of the day have been so much more drastically interrupted, by a house fire, a totalled automobile, injury, even death? Maybe that letter that had to be in the mail wasn't so important after all . . .


JULY 9

Emergencies do teach us that what we were doing that we thought was so important was nothing, really. Wouldn't it be great to be able to remember this in non-emergency situations?

The argument of the anti-nuclear weapons movement is that this is a true emergency, that nuclear war resulting in total annihilation of all life on this planet could in fact break out at any moment, maybe even by accident (computer error or failure).

This is essentially true, I believe. However, it falls into the category of the standing emergency (if one may create such outrageous categories), a kind of contradiction-in-terms that confuses all our normal patterns of response.

If the fire radio goes off I get up, throw on some clothes if it's the middle of the night, and drive to the fire station. But the danger of nuclear war is a siren sounding in our ears so constantly that we have no choice but to block it out, just to enable ourselves to respond . . . and then of course once we've blocked it out we often forget about responding. I know I do; other obligations, needs, interests, take priority.

For this new kind of emergency—24-hours-a-day, every day, potential consequences more drastic than even the death of your child, some real opportunities for action but still no relief in sight—we need a new kind of response. Jumping up and going to the fire station won't help. Jumping up and going to do some work at the local nuclear freeze office, or whatever, is more useful; but since it's a permanent, round-the-clock emergency, it makes more sense to be orderly about it, maybe commit yourself to be in that office one day a week, certain prearranged hours, doing volunteer work. Trouble is, that becomes a part of normal life, loses the flavor of emergency, and pretty soon the kids' soccer games, earning a living, and keeping your marriage together (or whatever) start to seem more important. And maybe they are. We have to live our lives. But then, damn it—what *is* the appropriate response?

JULY 11

A siren sounds in our ears so constantly that we have no choice but to block it out. And still it breaks through, and we hear the shrill warning and call to action, again and again, on and on. Maybe we do have another choice. This shrill alarm that penetrates everywhere doesn't respond to anything we try to do about it within the context of our dream. Maybe it's coming from outside the dream. Maybe it's trying to wake us up.

### July 12

And if we allow ourselves to be awakened?

### July 13

On the other side of all this fullness is a vast emptiness. We are ready to break through; we are very attracted to the unknown, that which is yet to be uncovered; and yet we hold back. We cling to the familiar, even while we yearn for what we have not yet touched.

On the other side of this sleep is the next wakening. The next moment of my life lies just outside the walls that define and protect *this* moment. Letting go of this moment and allowing the next to come on is certainly a little death.

On the other side of this orgasm is the new union. Would we be so willing to come if we knew what we were creating?

### July 14

A child shall lead us. We create our children, so that they will lead us out of here. We give birth to them, not so they will carry out our vision, but so they will carry on our process of envisioning.

Our highest transmission is not what we see but our ability to see. This is what we can pass on to the next generation.

### July 15

If we allow ourselves to be wakened, all the perils of the dream will be behind us in a moment.

We can escape from the nightmare.
Yes, but into what?
It is this question that holds us back.


### JULY 16

Where we are right now in our lives is familiar to us. No matter how uncomfortable it may have become, in many ways, still it has going for it the ultimate comfort of familiarity. We "know we can handle it." To move into an unfamiliar situation, no matter how promising, is always terrifying because we don't know if we can handle it. We *can't* know, until we get there, and then it will be too late to turn back.

So we stick with the familiar, even though we hate it. "Better the devil you know than the devil you don't know." Coming from such a point of view, who could hope to meet an angel?


### JULY 17

The appropriate response is to allow ourselves to feel and experience everything that exists in this moment. Including the standing emergency. Feel it. Breathe it in and breathe it out. Be calm. Allow your actions to arise naturally from your experience and your knowledge. Feel what you feel, experience what you experience, know what you know. No more, no less.

And now, without thinking about it, do what you do.

Feel your heart swell with unconditional love for everything that exists in this universe, and you will know that you have responded appropriately.


### JULY 18

I am not suggesting that love take the place of action. I am affirming that love is action, and that our actions can arise spontaneously from our love.

Do what you do. You are doing the right thing. The only obstacle is hesitation itself. And it's all right for there to be obstacles. Take your time. You are doing the right thing. Keep doing it!

I acknowledge that this is an expansive attitude. I could be embarrassed. Maybe I am. But damn it, it works! And it's not at all easy. Loving each other is the greatest challenge we've ever been faced with. But it is the appropriate response to the emergency, to our whole situation. We need to love who we are, so that we can allow ourselves to become who we are.

## July 19

Are we ready to become who we are? I don't know. But I know what the choice is . . .

## July 20

Our historic moment, our emergency, means just what the name implies: something is emerging. The new creature comes forth from the shell of the old. "I have set before you life and death, blessing and cursing: therefore choose life, that both thou and thy seed may live." (Deuteronomy, 30:19)

It takes courage to choose life, to say yes. We don't know what it is that emerges. We cannot know; we must choose blindly.

And yet, in a deeper sense there is nothing blind or unconscious about choosing to be who we are.

## July 21

It is time for the leap of faith.
Hold on tight.
Let go.

## JULY 22

Inspire. Expire.
Contract. Relax.
Hold tight. Let go.

## JULY 23

Let's go!

## JULY 24

It is a day like any other day. We do our breathing exercises. We raise our children. We reach out to touch our neighbors. We thank God to have been born into such a moment of great adventure. We feel despair, exhilaration, anger, fear, and love. We find something to do with our hands and minds. We eat, drink, sleep, and when we wake it is a day again. Moment gives birth to moment. We feel our own needs and the needs of those around us, and we respond as best we can.

## JULY 25

Standing with two or three other firemen on the back of a truck in the middle of the night is a kind of waking up together. The alarm went off in our separate houses, pulling us from sleep, and here we are racing through the night together. And where we're going, God only knows.

It's always kind of surprising to find yourself in the moment.

## JULY 26

Forgive me all my metaphors and analogies. I must say the same thing a hundred thousand different ways, until finally I hear it myself, and remember. And if I am the last to get the message, and everyone else has embraced it long since, then I will cross the finish line happily, knowing the rest of the race has already arrived.

## July 27

Now all the faces of the women I thought I loved have receded into uncertain memory. It's a perfectly nice day outside but I'd rather be in here with my pale flesh confronting the typewriter. My mind is empty. My bed is empty. The dishes are washed but the laundry still needs to be put away. My government still makes life more difficult for people in other places, Central America, giving guns to the handful of rich with which to threaten and sometimes slaughter the poor. I am not content.

The argument of the rich is that the poor are threatening *them*, trying to take away what is rightfully theirs.

And we who supply the guns, who loan money to the rich for our own profit, we who secretly support the enemies of freedom while proclaiming ourselves the symbol of freedom, we must look at this argument and cut through the confusions of politics and language and guilt and avoidance, and ask ourselves, what is right?

What is right is more important than what is practical.

## July 28

What is right is more important than what is practical.

## July 29

And I am responsible for the actions of my government. If *I* can't influence it, who can? If I won't, who will?

## July 30

Out of awareness comes responsibility, and out of responsibility comes action. To be aware of the suffering of others is to be to some extent responsible for it. No wonder we shut our eyes and cover our ears!

And the dilemma of our time is that it is possible now to be aware of so much. The murders of penniless Indian children in the highlands of Guatemala do not escape our attention, here in the cities and suburbs and small towns of electronic civilization.

Limits make service possible. I know well the boundaries of my small town fire protection district; I am not called to see and care for the mangled bodies of accident victims on roads outside our district. This allows me to stay with the job, to learn from it and be of service.

How shall we select the limits that will allow us to serve in this world community where there is so much more need than any one of us could ever respond to?

We need a new concept of response.


## JULY 31

We need to perform our acts of conscience, service, love and caring, within the context of a personal vision of the community we belong to and the world we are creating together.

With such a vision, mere duty (such as my duty to respond when the fire siren sounds) can become an act of love.

# Chapter Eight

# AUGUST

## AUGUST 1

When I was younger I wanted to wake people up. That was fun for a while. Now my purpose is a little different. I want to provide companionship, reassurance, support, stimulation to those who are already awakening.

"The great man fosters and takes care of superior men, in order to take care of all men through them," the *I Ching* tells us, in the hexagram called "Providing Nourishment." On an early Rolling Stones record, Mick Jagger paraphrases Solomon Burke: "Everybody here listen to my song tonight; gonna save the whole world."

When I was younger I wanted to save the whole world. I still do, although it's been a while since I dared to admit that. Basically I believe it's up to each one of us to choose whether we want the world to be saved or not. What is your vision? I'm not saying that you "should" want to save it. All I want's an honest answer.

"Everybody Needs Somebody to Love." That's the name of the song Mick Jagger was singing. Now we're waking up, and we don't want to be here alone. But at the same time we can't afford to be with someone else if they're not going to give us the space we need to go through what we're going through.

My vision is that by nourishing those who nourish others, I can touch and have an impact on the whole world. You can do the same thing. That's why I'm writing to you.

### AUGUST 2

I'm not writing to you because you have the *potential* to touch the world. I'm writing to you because you're already doing it, you're already sharing yourself, and I want to encourage you at your work.

### AUGUST 3

The challenge is to be completely in the moment when you touch another person. It doesn't require (and can't be achieved through) any kind of effort. All you have to do is not be holding on to anything.

### AUGUST 4

Of course, if you don't hold on, you might fall.

### AUGUST 5

And fall, and fall, and fall. It seems like this pit has no

bottom. And the more you try to get control and stop falling, the more anxious you become.

Might as well relax and enjoy it.

## AUGUST 6

Falling in love. When you fall in love, you usually find yourself letting go of a lot of things that you used to think were important. Or maybe you don't let go of those things, and you find yourself falling out of love again. It doesn't matter. It's completely up to you whether you choose to be in love or not. It has nothing to do with anyone else, regardless of what you or they may think.

I don't mean to be unromantic about this. Of course you need someone to fall in love with, and that person has to be worthy of your total attention. But they always are. The person you fall in love with is always worthy of your total attention. It's just up to you whether you choose to go on recognizing their worth or not.

And it's all right if you do, and it's all right if you don't. Regardless of how it may appear on the surface, whatever you choose to do will be just perfect for the rest of the universe. The only person you have to answer to is yourself.

I'm not saying, don't care about other people's feelings. The thing to do with other people's feelings is allow yourself to feel them, open yourself and be vulnerable and experience their feelings totally, let them become a part of you . . . and then go ahead and do what's right for you.

You have no way of knowing what's right for the other person. The most generous thing you can do is just not protect yourself against being aware of how they feel.

If you don't do what's right for you, you won't be doing what's right for anyone. You'll just be stuck in the middle making nobody happy, again.

## AUGUST 7

Sex is a bridge. In the act, an actual physical bridge is

created, across which living genetic information passes from one body to another. At the end of the act, one of the vessels involved contains and intermingles the essential identities of both separate beings. When we kiss with tongues in each other's mouths, we imitate the form of this bridge, we acknowledge the mystery and excitement of this connection with and into another entity. And when we practice birth control we engage in conscious paradox, striving for and protecting against at the same moment.

Male: wants to get in. Female: wants to be entered. This is the formula for union. Once the bridge is built, there is a great tendency for information to cross over it, and if the dice roll right a third entity begins to be formed and nurtured in the receptive vessel. The two become one become three. And isn't it remarkable how much this simple bit of architecture influences, even dominates, our lives?

### AUGUST 8

So sexual attraction is the desire to build a bridge. In the sense that it exists to make sure we reproduce ourselves, it is the desire to build a bridge to the future.

### AUGUST 9

No wonder this dumb instinct that fills our lives with so much pleasure, pain, and confusion, can be such a vehicle for awakening!

But in the same breath I am forced to admit that most of the time sex just puts us to sleep. It is a paradox, that my sexual desires do bring me to life and cause me to be more of who I am and take risks I would never consider otherwise, and yet at the same time my sexual desires also cause me to behave like an idiot, a rat in a cage pushing the button for pleasure helplessly over and over, trapped by a desire that never satisfies and never seems to go anywhere.

This paradox can be resolved, in theory, and, if we have the courage, maybe even in practice.

118

The fact is that the pursuit of satisfaction (sexual or otherwise) is an endless rat race. The more you get, the more you want. If your goal is satisfaction, you will never be satisfied. Lover after lover and still no love. After a while it isn't even fun any more.

This chasing after satisfaction represents an unwillingness to wake up. Let's say there's a little maze with a surprise package at the end. Fantasies of what might be in that package stimulate us tremendously, and we enter the maze to go and get it. At the same time, perhaps without consciously realizing it, we feel great fear of what might be in the package. Desire and fear very often go together. So we are driven by attraction and held back by repulsion.

So we play a little trick on ourselves. Halfway through the maze is a package that looks just like the package at the end of the maze that attracts us so. Since we're afraid of what might be in the real package, we plant this imitation package, just like the real thing except there's nothing in it. We enter the maze hungry with desire to reach the end and open the package. This never fails to stimulate us, and the adventure is on. Halfway through, we get to the false package. Our desire is to reach and open the package, and now we fulfill it. What pleasure, knowing we've gotten to the package and it is ours! What pleasure, unwrapping it and tearing it open. We did what we came to do, and we feel complete. Exhausted, we crawl out of the maze (bringing back nothing, since the package was empty). Next day, we look at the maze again and again feel an uncontrollable desire to go through it to the end and open the package and get what's in there. And again, our secret fear makes us stop halfway and open the false package that our mind tells us is absolutely the thing we wanted. And we believe it. We believe we want to open the package, to have the package, and we never admit that it's what's inside the package that's really driving us. So we avoid confronting our fears . . . at the expense of repeating the same incomplete act again and again and again.

And the more we deny that we have any fears, the more difficult it is to get out of the trap.

So the solution to the paradox is to speak that terrible truth: that sex is not an end in itself. What really drives us is (take your choice): the desire for awakening, the desire to be more of who I am, the desire to be vulnerable, the desire to have children. The desire to go beyond where I am, and build a bridge to the future, the unknown. The desire to have something happen that is bigger than me, outside my control, the desire to take a meaningful risk, a real risk, the desire to surrender to the will of God.

"Uh huh," says the mind, "that sounds great. Of course I want those things, or some of them, anyway." But the mind is lying. Insofar as the desire is to open the package, embrace the unknown, take a step beyond what the mind can control . . . the mind doesn't want that. Or maybe it does, but it's willing to just have the wanting—to pretend that having and acting out the desire is the same as fulfilling it. The mind will go to any extreme to avoid surrendering control.

The mind loves the trip but it doesn't want to get there. Sexual desire is the desire to create or discover something new. Mind loves to pursue that desire, always making sure that what's at the end of the road will only seem to be new, will in fact be under the control of the mind.

But every now and then sex takes us out of and beyond our minds. And then, thank God, we find ourselves in trouble, in the terrifying uncertainty and newness that is what we wanted all along.

### August 10

Beyond the barriers of control, lies conception. Only then is the bridge completed. Only then can the baby be born.

### August 11

It is true that the words "baby" and "conception" can be taken metaphorically. Sexual desire is the desire to create or discover something new . . . and we don't necessarily know what that "something" is. To say that sex is only for making babies would be to contradict and deny some of my most profound experiences.

At the same time, it is misleading to believe that sex can ever be wholly separated from baby-making. Even when there is no physical possibility of conception, the fact is that when we are making love our bodies understand us to be joined together in the act of reproduction. The statistical probability of a "successful" outcome does not affect the body's understanding of the purpose of the act . . . not even when the probability is zero.

This can lead to serious problems of communication between mind and body, because the mind does consider the statistical probability of a particular outcome a very important piece of information.

Mind quite properly believes it has a responsibility to exercise conscious control over outcomes—that is, the future—to the extent that it is able. If we recognize abstinence as a form of birth control (the most effective form, in fact), we can easily see that birth control is one of the mind's primary responsibilities, even in nonhuman species (wherever there is sexual choice and sexual rejection, as seems true among most birds and animals, some sort of "mind" may be said to be functioning; instinct alone would not provide sufficient differentiation).

The body, on the other hand, is designed to maximize its own reproductive ability during its fertile years. There are physiological modifiers on this process, for example changes in hormone production and balance, but still it is not inaccurate to see the body, in any sexual encounter (even rape), as always striving to conceive.

Body's actions could probably be influenced by mind's input if mind and body were in good communication—but alas that seems to be the exception among us rather than the rule. Mind and body, based on the experience each has had in the past, tend not to trust each other. As a result, mind usually practices birth control by direct intervention (as opposed to conferring with the body to reach consensus).

Body's reaction to this intervention is to try to circumvent it, if possible.

And so the struggle begins; and where it will end, neither mind nor body can guess.

## August 12

I think it is important to notice that part of the excitement of sex, similar to the excitement of auto-racing or mountain-climbing or other death-defying activities, is the possibility of irreversible consequences. In this respect, to be afraid of sex is no more crazy than to be afraid of hang-gliding. An hour's dalliance could change the course of your life forever, and not necessarily for the better.

The fact that we are taking a real risk (of conceiving, of having to have an abortion, of giving birth to a being for whom we will always bear some responsibility . . . or of course the alternate possibility of becoming emotionally attached beyond what we might have chosen or planned) heightens the excitement, gives us a real sensation of being alive. Flirting with creating life is similar to flirting with death: we are thrilled and terrified at the prospect of the irreversible.

## August 13

My own prejudice is that trouble is better than safety, if one must have one or the other, because trouble is going somewhere. Uncertainty means being alive; certainty is death. "In landlessness alone resides the highest truth," as Mr. Melville told us.

Of course, I don't always practice what I preach. And the part of me that seeks security, knowing it is subject to challenge if recognized, is clever enough to keep many of its operations quite invisible to my eye.

Friends and strangers can see how the desire for security motivates me, much more clearly (often) than I can see it myself.

## August 14

This problem is also an opportunity. At any given moment I can (if kissed or kicked hard enough) penetrate my own smugness and open to the universe again by uncovering the operations of the security forces at work inside me. This is painful (just when I thought I had everything handled!) but it does give me room to breathe.

## AUGUST 15

Suddenly I feel lost. What is it I've been trying to say in these last few pages? What is it I've been trying to say in this whole book? I haven't the slightest idea. You laugh, but this is a very scary (and very familiar) position for the author to find himself in. The only way out that I know of is to let go of all of it, and find out what if anything I'd like to say right now.

## AUGUST 16

I'd like to say a prayer.

I pray for the courage to swallow my pride, not once but over and over again.

I pray for the people all over the world who are tyrannized and trapped by political and economic power struggles.

I pray for the children, that they have a world to grow up in and the opportunity to create something with their lives.

I pray for love, love to give, love to give every day, to my family friends lovers co-workers and every person in my life.

I pray for the aspirations of all beings, whenever those aspirations are in harmony with what is right.

I pray for energy and discrimination, that I may always do and choose to do the joyous work that is right in front of me.

I pray for laughter and friendship.

## AUGUST 17

"If your goal is satisfaction, you will never be satisfied."

It's like form without content. The absence of content leaves us unfulfilled, and we reach for more, again and again, meanwhile feeling emptier and emptier. True satisfaction, satisfaction that satisfies, can only come when we reach for something bigger than our own pleasure. Then, each particle of progress gives us satisfaction, because what we've done means something, it makes a difference.

Our lives have content when our actions have a purpose. Content means to contain something. We are vessels. Our purpose here, regardless of whether we are "men" or "women," is both to empty ourselves and to let ourselves be filled.

My power only feels like it's mine when I'm using it in service to something greater than me. My own lack of humility most days shows me how little I understand this sentence.


## AUGUST 18

What is greater than me? What is bigger than my own pleasure? Whatever it is, it's with me all the time. And I'm afraid of it. I'm afraid that if I surrender control, there will be nothing left of me. And as many times as I've done that, and that hasn't happened, still I find it so difficult to let go. I have a thousand tricks for crawling back into my shell. One of my tricks is to talk as though I understand these things.


## AUGUST 19

Don't be fooled. I'm not talking at all. You're the one who's talking, and I'm writing it down.


## AUGUST 20

What would you like to say next? I am your instrument; use me. It's funny—I said at the start of this chapter that I didn't want to wake people up, I wanted to serve as a companion and offer support to those who are already awakening.

And then I found myself writing the most challenging material (for me) in the book, the stuff about sex and babies and reaching for false satisfaction. When I wrote it, I felt very excited, like this was something I'd always wanted to look at and put in words, and at last I've done it. But now, a week or two later, I feel so confused and threatened by it all that I wonder if I should remove it from the book, go back and make a fresh start on this chapter? And then I think, no, that material should stay in, it'll wake people up. Hah . . .

It's true: I don't want to wake you up, or "fix" your problems. I'd rather have you like me, and enjoy spending time with me. And yet, I have this terrible tendency to start giving advice. Suddenly I am reminded of how I always wanted to raise my hand and display my knowledge in junior high school. I was a know-it-all, a show-off, and it took a long time for me to realize my indulgence was causing me more pain than pleasure . . . and an even longer time before I was able to do anything about it. And here I am again. Funny how it never really changes.

Am I trying to wake myself up? Yeah, probably. And probably I'd do much better to let go of it and just be my own companion and let myself know it's worthwhile to be as awake as I already am. Instead of forcing myself into resistance, I could be giving me the support I deserve.

## AUGUST 21

It occurs to me that when I was younger I would have said that waking people up is far more important than having them like you . . . indeed, it was a great fear of mine that my desire to be liked, my need for approval, might deflect me from my purpose, might stop me from telling people the truth.

And I still find it very easy to slip back to that point of view: that my purpose is to speak the truth, and that the desire for approval is the greatest enemy of that purpose, the greatest obstacle to honesty. Remember Jonah? God told him to speak the truth to his people, and he ran as fast and far as he could in the other direction. He didn't want the responsibility. I can relate to that, and so it was easy for me to construct a romantic image of myself as a prophet speaking out, regardless of the risk, and telling people what they don't want to hear. I could even see myself, like Jonah, as someone who ran away and then ultimately came back (you can run but you cannot hide) to do God's work.

But . . . sometimes my romantic self-images are another complicated defense against accepting my own power and being who I am and fulfilling my purpose. Just one more (subtle) place to hide.

You see, I always believed (pretended?) that my purpose was to *speak* the truth. And my familiar line, when people came to acknowledge me, was always, "It's not me; it's the words."

Or I'd tell them: "It's you. I wrote the words; you put the meaning into them."

True enough. And the reason that I'm finally starting to see that I can serve my purpose better by being with people than by advising them, is I'm starting to acknowledge that it's the power of my presence, in the room or on the page, that encourages people to put meaning into the words. My presence. Being, not speaking. What a terrifying truth for me to have to face. What a rude awakening.

### AUGUST 22

It's as though a bodyworker were told that it's not all the techniques he (or she) has learned that make the difference, not even her innate talent and sense of where and when and how to touch, but just the power of her presence that heals people. And all those techniques and talents simply serve to guide that power and make it more available. (Or else they serve to hide the power, and make it unavailable, when we get so concerned about technique that we fail to be there for the other person.)

Being, not doing. Why is it so scary? Why do I feel comfortable to be seen as a person who does powerful deeds, and

126

uncomfortable to be seen as a person who simply is powerful, has power? Among other things, I think I have a belief that it's all right to get credit for what I do, but not for what I am.

### AUGUST 23

Put it another way: I don't want to be powerful. I'm much more comfortable imagining I'm an un-powerful person who happens to do some powerful things.

### AUGUST 24

I just remembered that one of my goals for this year is to be more at home with my power. If the world is going to transform and be a better place for human beings and all living creatures, this is something we all need to do. I don't think there's anyone reading this book who isn't playing some sort of game of pretending not to be powerful. And how can we let our power serve us, serve all of us, if we won't even acknowledge that it's there?

We think that if we don't admit it's there, it won't burn us. And we get burned anyway, and blame it on God, or the other person, or the government, or the general situation. If we'd only admit how powerful we are, maybe we could improve the situation at the source.

Now that's a responsibility that's bigger than telling the truth to people. Who among us is ready and willing to respond to the truth about ourselves?

### AUGUST 25

I'm willing to be with you for the value it may have for you. Am I willing to be with you for the value it may have for me?

## August 26

If you want to be loved, give yourself away. Be willing to smile. Remember why you came here.

How am I to remember these things? I will write them in sand, on the tide flat, and take a deep breath of ocean air.

## August 27

Our purpose is to empty ourselves and let ourselves be filled. And that's called breathing. How can this be the solution to all our problems? And yet it is.

I feel restless, insecure, overwhelmed, exhausted, unwilling, unworthy, courageous, committed, and ready to go the distance. I am a pack of contradictions that work together to create whatever it is I contribute: this mess is my beauty, take it or leave it. Who you see is who I am.

## August 28

There is always a new morning, and every sunrise allows us the opportunity to start fresh again. It isn't necessary for me to consciously carry around everything I've written in this book so far (and have it all clear in my head before I write another word), just as it isn't necessary for me to carry around conscious awareness of everything I've done in my life up to now in order to take my next breath. All that stuff is in me anyway, and I am who I am and the book is what it is as we breathe and write in the moment.

To be conscious of here and now is enough. Stopping the moment while we try to take inventory of all our pasts and futures doesn't work so well.

## August 29

Faith in myself means to know that I am here, and all I have to do is allow myself to be here. The instant I do that, the moment I let go of what I'm holding onto, I find myself at the center of the universe again. All I need to do for my son is be here with him. Isn't it funny how we try everything else but that?

**August 30**

I also would like a little companionship, reassurance, support, stimulation as I wake up alone here. And I think for the first time in a long time I'm willing to ask for that.

**August 31**

Thank you for encouraging me at my work.

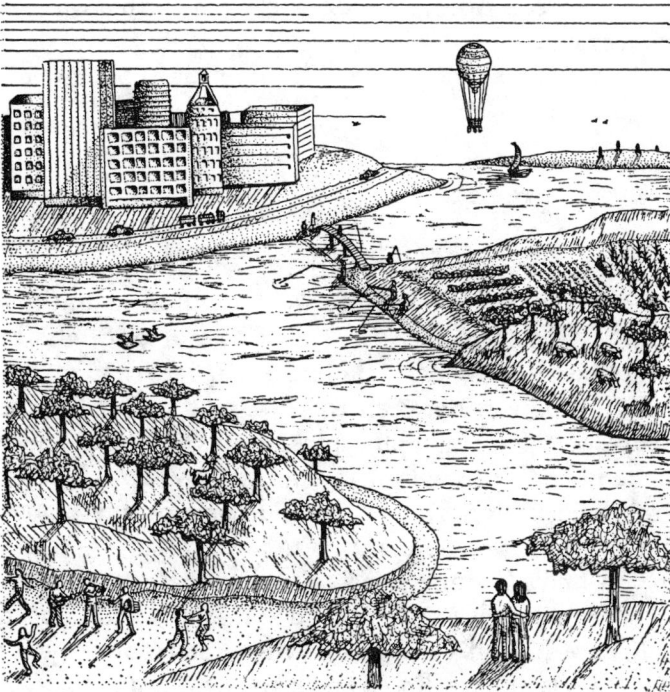

# Chapter Nine

# SEPTEMBER

**SEPTEMBER 1**

It it easier to reach out for something new than to complete what's already here. But one thing stops me: the certain knowledge that if I reach and capture the new thing, sooner or later (probably sooner, the way things have been going lately) I'm gonna be in the exact same position I am right now. All that effort, just to end up back here again. Maybe I'm better off sitting still (no! I can't do it!) and experiencing the pain of being incomplete. Maybe if I can just hold on for

131

a few more centuries, a door will open in this wall of rock that faces me.

And maybe this time I'll have the courage to walk through the door.

## SEPTEMBER 2

Because this happens to be the 20th century, I have a telephone and an automobile. Wow. I can pick up the phone and be talking to another person. I have a lot of choice. The automobile also gives me choice, about where I am, who I'm with. What power. Between the first sentence and the second sentence of this paragraph I picked up the phone and talked with someone with whom I have a very close relationship (that I don't understand at all) and had not one but a series of unexpected experiences and I'm not the same person I was. And you know, I don't need to understand or remember any of this. It's enough that I needed something and I got it, I let myself have it, and I can acknowledge her power (what a resource she is in my life!) and my own. And I got what I needed. Some other century, I'd have done the same thing some other way. We are who we are, even as the props change around us.

## SEPTEMBER 3

If I acknowledge this power I have, all doors open to me. My weakness, my sickness disappear. Women reach out to me; I have my choice of pleasures. And I can go on with my work.

It sounds so simple.

And it is. And what I can learn from my hesitation is: I am afraid of open doors. I am afraid of strength and health. I am afraid of women who reach for me; I am afraid of having pleasure.

And in the end, it is only my drive to go on with my work that sets me free.

## September 4

Now I can feel something inside me awakening.

## September 5

What an extraordinary, invisible struggle our lives are! And when you look at a person, the struggles you can see, the struggles they reveal to themselves and the world, are usually only a clever disguise for what is really going on.

For example, I spoke yesterday to my friend "A." She has been involved since I've known her in a tremendous on-going struggle with herself about whether the man she loves and lives with is right for her. There are a million variations on this, and it absorbs her totally. And in no way is it the real issue. The real issue for her is the power she has, and whether she is willing to use it—not in her love relationship, particularly, but in her work, her relationship with the world.

And she knows. Isn't that interesting! She acknowledged on the phone that everything is different for her the moment she leaves the town she lives and grew up in, even for an evening. And she acknowledged that her boyfriend wants them, wants her, to move. And that she is definitely not ready or willing, as much as she hates her situation she hangs on to it fiercely, and not out of ignorance. She knows. So when she feels hate for her situation she gets angry at herself. Then she sees herself getting angry and hates herself for *that*. And tries to stop. And even gives up alcohol, and smoking (and sex, sometimes), to prove her power.

But she won't leave town and make things easy for herself.

Why? Because of fear, fear of the unknown? No. Fear is not a reason, it is an instrument by which we manipulate ourselves. "I can't, because of my fear." Not true. The true statement, too naked for us to say most times, is, "I won't."

## September 6

Why? Why won't I, if not because of fear?

Because if I do take the next step in my life, someone's going to expect something of me. And I'm not willing to accept that burden.

I'd rather be unhappy and sick and never get what I want than be tricked into accepting more responsibility during my visit here, this lifetime.

Fuck you, God.

### SEPTEMBER 7

Like it or not, this is what we are really saying with our lives, most of the time. And it can be a very heroic stance (cf. most of western literature). This is what the struggle is about.

And it doesn't offer much comfort to know that the only way to win is to surrender.

### SEPTEMBER 8

Maybe (I'm serious now) we win by having the nuclear holocaust. That'll show God He can't intimidate us!

Death before dishonor.

When I asked you whether you want the world to be saved, it was not an idle question. And the last thing I want to do is give the impression that it's obvious which answer is right, and which is wrong.

I say, "choose life"—and yet the truth is I notice it's an ongoing struggle, for me as much as anyone else, to make this choice. Why can't I make it once and get it over with?

### SEPTEMBER 9

Answer: because to "get it over with" is to choose death. And that's the killer: when you choose life, the choices—the struggle—never end. To choose life is to choose to go on choosing. Who among us would not get angry, tired, resentful? Who invented this stupid game, anyway? I've half a mind to quit while I'm ahead . . .

## September 10

Honor the struggle. It is real. It is our fate. And there are no easy answers.

## September 11

I am not on this planet to get something done. That's a misunderstanding I think I've been laboring under most of my life. But right at this moment anyway it seems clear to me that I wasn't sent here to "do" something. My purpose, anyone's purpose, cannot be objectified. I don't think it's correct to speak of Einstein's achievements and then say, in hindsight, "the reason this man lived was to do these things." I need to look at it a different way: the man had a purpose, and the things he happened to accomplish (the ones we're aware of, and remember and appreciate) are expressions of that purpose . . . and, for Einstein and for all of us, these deeds are always ultimately frustratingly incomplete expressions of the vision we see, the spirit that drives us. I don't limit this to great thinkers, artists, leaders. Every one of us is here for a reason, if anyone is. It's all or nothing: either there is no purpose to the whole mess or else purpose flows and pulses through every grain of sand and every action and interaction in the known and unknown universe. Including me and my actions, and you and yours.

So I'm taking a position, and my position (for the moment) is that life has meaning and there is a reason why we're here. "We" collectively and also we as individuals, you and me. And I'm saying that I'm not here to accomplish anything, there's nothing I have to do. Nothing I "have to" do. Nothing I have to "do." And it's fine for me to do things, in fact given my purpose I can't help but do things. But that's a side-effect, really. My purpose is to be here. Because I'm here, things happen, things get done, or undone. But my job is not to "do." Doing is secondary. My job is to be.

135

## SEPTEMBER 12

When I say (usually very secretly and invisibly and indirectly) "Fuck you, God!", I am not really saying that I refuse to do what I think God wants me to do. What I'm really saying is I refuse to be who God and I both know I am.

## SEPTEMBER 13

And I am that person anyway. So I'm not fooling anybody. All I'm doing is pretending to be invisible by sticking my head in the sand.

## SEPTEMBER 14

When I have my head in the sand I have my ass in the air. Sometimes it's pretty funny to walk around and see a whole planet full of people with their asses sticking up in the air. And sometimes it's sad. Who are we pretending to hide from?

How about on the count of three, we all pull our heads from the sand and admit that we are who we are? Ready? One . . . two . . . three.

## SEPTEMBER 15

It doesn't matter whether there's a God or not. The truth is, if you think it matters, or if you think it matters how we talk about Her, or Him, you are just trying to confuse the issue. Arguing about God is a way of hiding from God. Working for God can be a great way of hiding from God. So can looking for God. And if you say God doesn't exist, or that you don't know what I mean by the word, that's fine: give me another word and I'll use that instead.

The truth is, we fight about language so we won't have to listen to what each other are saying.

We are always telling each other what we already know; and we purposely misunderstand so we won't have to hear it.

### September 16

Because if I hear (and let myself be touched by) what I already know, I might have to remember that I already know it.

And then, who knows?, it might get harder for me to fritter away my life pretending there's something I need to find out.

### September 17

And again this morning death called me out of bed and slapped me in the face. The fire siren went off at seven A.M. and we responded to an "injury accident" on the country road that winds out of town. When we got to the scene there was nothing to do. The car had obviously flown through the air, severed a tree, and landed near the creek, where it had stayed for hours waiting for the sun to come up and someone to notice the wreckage. A young father and his six-year-old son were dead in the car.

I cried at the scene and I'm crying now. It's a release, a way for the body to let out emotions that turn to poison otherwise. I only wish I could cry louder and longer. Yesterday a commercial airliner with hundreds of people aboard was shot down for violating another country's airspace, and the smell of war was in the air for a moment. And we sit here passively and hear the news and how are we to release what we feel?

### September 18

We are breathing in all the time. What gets us stuck, trapped, in our lives and emotions, is that sometimes we forget to breathe out again.

### September 19

I've been on the road, I've been falling in love again, I've been away from my typewriter for a week or more and now I'm sitting here because I want to keep going, I want to feel like I'm making progress, I want to write and the only problem is I feel very unwilling to say anything.

What a familiar feeling, to be sitting here desperately wanting to talk and yet flatly refusing to open my mouth.

I claim to want to write about some or all of the thousand things that run through my attention. Well, here's my chance. And I really don't know what's stopping me.

It's like I'm holding my breath, refusing to breathe out, refusing to let the natural process take its course. When the writing does come, I don't have to push it; it flows out by itself. That suggests that when it doesn't come, something is blocking the flow. Maybe I'm not willing to be naked right now. Maybe I think I've got something to lose.


## SEPTEMBER 20

This morning my wife asked me again to write to her sister in Japan to explain my "side" of what's going on, our separation. Her sister requested this, more than a month ago, and I've been wanting to comply but finding it difficult. Wanting to but not wanting to. The problem is, I don't know what's going on, exactly—I could just talk about that, but it would be subtle and hard to translate, and I don't know who would be doing the translation. And what I find is I'm not really willing to put down on paper, for my wife to read, my thoughts about where we are right now, the form and possible future of our relationship. It's like, anything I say may be used against me.

I asked my wife if she would write a letter to me today, telling me what she feels is going on. She said no, or that she would write one only if I wrote one at the same time. That cleared things up for me, because I realize that I feel the same way, and that the letter to her sister would be me sticking out my neck while my spouse takes no risks. Anyway, when I realize that we're both unwilling to write such a letter for the other to see, I don't feel guilty any more about not writing it.

And I notice she brought up the subject just before she

138

had to leave for work, so we wouldn't be able to talk about it too much. Hmm, she's as protected as I am.

### SEPTEMBER 21

You may notice from reading between the lines of the last section that my spouse and I are separated but living in the same house (much of the time). It's quite a small house, too. Well, the ways of men and women are endlessly fascinating. Our excuse is we don't have the money to get her another place, and that as long as we don't fight (we've been fairly good about that lately) it's nice for the boys to have both of us around a lot.

I know I don't want to be any *less* separated than we are (no desire to see us together again as lovers, or as husband and wife in the eyes of the world). I'm not sure whether I have any strong desire for us to be more separated, either. Another dwelling, more space, would be nice—I mean another one in addition to the one we have. Separate incomes, separate accounts, is already happening, and more of that would be just fine. But it's perfectly nice to have her around, as long as we're not criticizing each other or telling each other what to do. And it's even happening that sometimes I can listen to and learn from things she says about me that once I would have reacted to automatically, shutting out the content and responding only to the fact that I think I've been criticized. I still do that, but not every time. Some of my defenses are falling. And I'd say that she's also opening to me to about the same degree.

In some ways, by "separating" we're making more space to be together. It just takes a lot of time and patience to work out the details.

### SEPTEMBER 22

Men and women are an extraordinary challenge to each other, because of the vulnerability we create in each other. Whether it's love or sex or children or the pragmatic details of sharing lives, money, space, time, the fact is that the intimate nature of our interactions puts us in touch with each other's weaknesses as well as our strengths. Indeed, one of the reasons we get together is we need to be able to share those weaknesses, those vulnerable places. There is this real and beautiful impulse to open up and be naked with another person. Alas there is also the instinct of self-protection, self-preservation, which causes us to quietly stockpile our knowledge of the other person to use as a defensive or offensive weapon just in case they ever start "misusing" what they know about us. Balance of power. Balance of terror, very often. With our lovers, with our mates, we are stronger and weaker than we are with anyone else. So the study of ourselves in our relationships is the study of ourselves when we're most being who we really are.

And for that very reason, this tends to be the part of our lives where we are most blind to what we are doing and who we are being.

## SEPTEMBER 23

We need love, we need sex, we need to raise children, many of us, and we need and want to share our lives, our money, our space, our time. We want intimacy, vulnerability, we want and need the opportunity to open to another person and experience ourselves being as powerful and beautiful and playful and alive as we really are.

And we all know from experience that if we let ourselves want something or someone "too much" we are putting ourselves at risk of terrible pain, confusion, disappointment, anger, hatred and self-hatred, if and when we find ourselves unable to "have" what we want so much. Experience tells us it is easier to keep the lid of the box shut than to try to close it again once it has been opened. We're scared, in other words. and based on our personal experience of what has happened before, we have every reason to be scared. We can't trust ourselves. That's not nice to say, but it tends to be true in terms of what we've experienced. Or if we don't want to admit that we can't trust ourselves, we put the blame on others and say

140

that men, or women, are no damn good and we're afraid of being hurt by one of them again.

Desire and fear do battle with each other, and even when desire wins fear is always waiting in the wings.

And yet our needs won't allow us to rest.

## SEPTEMBER 24

What is the answer? There is no answer. Why can't I just choose life once and get it over with? Because getting it over with is death. Enlightenment is death. Awakening sounds like something extraordinary that happens to a person once in a lifetime. But actually our human experience of awakening is that we must do it again each morning. We go to sleep. We wake up.

Even when you've found a person to stay with and be with and live with, you have to rediscover and recreate intimacy with that person again and again, and each time you have to take a terrible risk to do so. It doesn't get any easier. It doesn't get any safer.

## SEPTEMBER 25

Waking up together is what we do each day. We wake up on this planet and there's all these other people and creatures here with us. We can reach over and embrace them or we can turn our backs. And we can't decide the night before. We have to choose anew at each moment.

If we don't choose anew at each moment, our embrace becomes by definition an automatic response, and not an embrace at all.

## SEPTEMBER 26

And if your position is that there's a right choice, and you're trying to get to a state of consciousness where you'll make the right choice every time, forget it. That's death.

Preconceptions about which choice is right can lead to having no choice at all. I mean, of course we always have preconceptions. But we have to let go of them (not destroy them, just let go of them) at the moment of choosing.

My marriage died for me when I'd been embraced so many times out of duty that I couldn't believe the real thing any more.

## SEPTEMBER 27

Men and women not trusting each other is like the Americans not trusting the Russians, and vice versa. It's not irrational. Each of these parties has excellent reasons not to trust the other, based on personal experience. The challenge for our era is to find the means by which they (we) can choose to trust each other even though these things that have happened all have happened (and will certainly happen again).

What a surrender that would take, to trust even with the conscious knowledge that we have been betrayed and will be betrayed again!

It's almost like, we have to go beyond "trust," because trust can be defined as the conviction that one will not be betrayed. So in place of trust we need love, love not conditioned on or affected by anything in the past or the future.

Is there such a thing, is it possible?

Yes. God's love is not conditional.

And the challenge of waking up together at this time in human history is that exactly in this sense we must mature and become more Godlike: for our own survival, we as individual nations and individual men and women, humans, must learn to practice God's love, unconditional love.

## SEPTEMBER 28

Can you imagine what a damn-fool thing it would be, for the Americans and the Russians to choose to love each other unconditionally? (Particularly after both sides have humiliated each other publicly so many times.)

Let's face it, we'd rather destroy the planet than act like fools in front of God and everybody.

### SEPTEMBER 29

Or maybe we wouldn't. Let's not prejudge the issue. While we breathe, we are still free to choose, and choose again.

### SEPTEMBER 30

So the question for you and me is: what are the limits on my power to love? Am I willing to take the risk of discovering that there are no limits?

# Chapter Ten

# OCTOBER

## OCTOBER 1

This book is full of questions, and I can think of a thousand more. Here's one: am I willing to be surrounded by friends? And the answer seems to be, yes, more willing than I ever have been before.

This seems to be a very important aspect of planetary awakening: the willingness to see nearby beings (i.e., other parts of the system of which you are a part) (system = living organism, in the sense that we are each a part or cell of a vast living organism, now identified by us as "the biosphere of

Earth" though its limits may extend far beyond what even that phrase suggests) as friendly, benevolent . . . the willingness to be surrounded by friends.

It's not easy. It's called intimacy . . . and it is demanding. The most difficult part of waking up together—and also the greatest reward—is intimacy.

"Awakening" suggests that the intimacy (of being part of this living creature, of having its other living extensions all around) is not new; what is new, and demanding, is the need to be *conscious* of the intimacy, to know that it is happening.

Awakening means becoming more conscious: conscious of ourselves as extensions or elements of a living being, surrounded by other extensions.

Conscious of, awake to, our intimacy with God.

### OCTOBER 2

The reason I can write the crazy way I do is that each level of reality (or of our understanding) is in fact a metaphor for or analogue of the other levels; this happens to be the way that "meaning" (understanding) (reality) is organized.

In other words, things (or words) that look like each other have something to do with each other.

Human science didn't rediscover the ancient knowledge that things that look like each other have something to do with each other until the advent of genetics, sometime in the last century. That's okay. We all spend our lives rediscovering things . . . often the same things over and over. And as we are individually, so are we collectively, and so the human race spends its time under the sun rediscovering again and again what it has always known.

Right now I think we are waking up again to the great discovery that it's okay for us to be here.

### OCTOBER 3

I can write the way I do because: (a) I am waking up again to the awareness that it's okay for me to be here, to be who I am, and (b) because each level of reality is in fact a metaphor for all other levels. So if I pick a phrase like "waking up together," it will be the case that all the different images the phrase suggests will resonate with and cast light on each other.

It is true that when two people are waking up together, they experience intimacy (even when they deny it). So if personal awakening is analogous to planetary awakening, which I believe to be true, and if the image of two lovers waking up together is a metaphor that casts light on all situations of awakening, then my knowledge that the challenge for lovers is intimacy suggests to me that this must also be the challenge in my relationship with God (personal awakening) and in the issues facing us collectively as humans (planetary awakening).

In other words, one thought leads to another. An analogy for a writer is like an experiment for a scientist: a fun place, an awkward place, a place where a bit of truth (whatever that is) may sometimes be revealed.

## OCTOBER 4

And I intercut analogy with occasional acknowledgment of the personal reality around me—like for example I could tell you I watched two soccer games this morning at the same time on adjacent fields (a dutiful and excited father) —because it's a way of grounding myself, my reader, my book. It brings me back to the moment. As a writer and as a person I am constantly looking for techniques that will help bring me back to what's going on right now.

## OCTOBER 5

Otherwise I get lost in the analogies, mirrors within mirrors.

By contemplating reality I lose touch with what's real. Oh well . . .

See? I just can't stop playing with words. I think I'd better go to bed now.

147

## OCTOBER 6

Isn't it interesting that I sit out here in this office and I play with words and I play with myself and yet I don't think of myself as a playful person?

## OCTOBER 7

There is a person who has come into my life in the last few weeks who is putting me back in touch with my playfulness. It's wonderful. She's wonderful. And at the same time she helps me be comfortable with and more effective in my purpose, my work. And her influence also seems to be causing progress for me in areas where I feel incomplete: communication with my wife, managing my debts, cleaning up my house.

Her name is Donna, and I must admit that nothing quite this intense has happened to me since my interaction with Judith, almost a year ago.

Judith accepted me, embraced me, opened me. And rejected me. All perfect. When I am truly honest, I know that she accepted and embraced who I really am, and then rejected my efforts to use her as a place to hide from who I am. Her actions toward me were impeccable.

"Judith" means "she who praises He-who-is."

## OCTOBER 8

"Donna" means lady, feminine of lord, "she whose power and grace are to be respected," a representative of the divine in human form.

If you believe in the cosmic significance of puns, as I do, you'll notice that her name also means "gift."

I reached a point in this manuscript, this story, where I announced that for the first time in a long time I felt willing to ask for "a little companionship, reassurance, support, stimulation as I wake up alone here." Donna arrived very soon thereafter.

148

Be careful what you ask for. It may be given to you, and then you will be forced to come to terms with your own willingness or unwillingness to receive.

## OCTOBER 9

My heart is an open book. And all I have to do is remember to breathe.

## OCTOBER 10

I continue to have experiences of what I call "the midnight hour" and I continue to find it very difficult to say anything about these experiences. I wonder why I once wanted to write a whole book on the subject? I guess as a way of saying to myself and anyone else who might be interested that this is a major theme in my life.

When my lady and I stay up most of the night, talking and making love, this is the essence of the midnight hour. We create a special place around ourselves that is close and intimate and timeless and infinite. I notice that we create it with our enthusiasm for each other, which leads into a mutual willingness and eagerness to share each other's enthusiasm for life, the universe. My long drives alone, surrounded by music (cassettes), up and down the California and Oregon coasts, stopping at every vista point, are also experiences of the midnight hour. So is playing Go on the beach at Santa Monica with my old friend Rick. We talk, we don't talk. One is with lovers, friends, strangers, alone. There are no specific words to describe the midnight hour.

## OCTOBER 11

I wanted to travel and I urgently wanted to go to an annual week-long gathering of old friends and interesting strangers, on the other side of the continent, and at the last moment I had to cancel and it took me days and days to let go of my disappointment and breathe out my expectations. And when I finally got back from not having gone anywhere, the midnight hour knocked on my door, came calling unplanned, unannounced and unexpected, with an intensity I can hardly remember experiencing before, and I'm so glad it found me at home.

## OCTOBER 12

It's so hard to let go of what we think we want—so hard to believe that we have to breathe out before we can breathe in again.

The challenge is to dream great dreams and let go of them, throw them away when the time comes whether they seem to have served their purpose or not.

The dreams can't be born again until you let them die. Let go.

## OCTOBER 13

It isn't easy.

## OCTOBER 14

It's hard for us to distinguish between the act of visualizing, on the one hand, and the condition of holding on to the pictures we have in our minds. What's the difference? The difference is we are alive in the act, and dead in holding onto the shell the act leaves behind.

A lot of us think we're practicing visualization when in fact we only practiced it once, and ever since we've been holding tight to the images we saw that one time. Holding tight to the images, while seemingly a natural extension of visualizing, does us no good. It is only the act itself—the moment when we are *seeing*—that is powerful. Holding on to the image just delays the moment when we will *see* again.

150

## October 15

What we can *see* we can have. If we want to live in a world with freedom and justice for all, we can't just say it, we have to *see* it. If we want our children to grow up in a world free from the threat of nuclear holocaust, it is more important to *see* such a world in our minds and hearts than it is to know how to get there.

If we *see* clearly enough and persevere in this (not holding on to the image but instead creating it from nothing over and over again), the getting there will take care of itself. The world we envision will come to us, because we have made space for it to exist.

## October 16

I am not suggesting that those who merely sit and daydream are superior to or are somehow accomplishing more than those who toil in the fields. First, this *seeing* I speak of is rigorous, demanding work; anyone can do it, and each of us is ready to do it now with no further preparation, but it's not the sort of thing that can be completed in an afternoon of good intentions or even an intensive weekend workshop. It's not the sort of thing that can be completed at all, in fact; *seeing* the world as whole and healthy is a lifetime commitment and undertaking and not only must we practice it, we must share it with our contemporaries and pass it on to our descendants.

And second, those who sit and daydream and claim that the world will transform as soon as other people change and agree to follow my plan, are not seers at all. They are only pretenders, waiters, and though they don't know it they are waiting for their own awakening, not anyone else's. Because to *see* is to see oneself as part of the world, to see oneself moving and interacting with the whole, acknowledging your own power to make the whole universe work by choosing, voluntarily and consciously, to do what you are here to do. So that the true dreamer, true visionary, is always toiling in some field or other, and joyously. We know what we are

151

creating, even when we don't know how we do it. We *see* the whole, and so our work proceeds in that direction as we modestly and confidently transform reality together.

And remember, you are doing this already. I am here only to remind you to reaffirm your vision. All the doubts, confusions, terrors, awkward beginnings and repeated stumblings are simply proof that we are not hiding from this process; we are allowing it to take place.

## OCTOBER 17

And when we encounter obstacles in the process, one difficult but very effective approach is to let our dreams die, let go of what we think we want. This works because you cannot lose what is part of you, what is truly yours. So there is no need to hold on to what you truly have, and no reason to hold on to anything else.

Letting go is not saying yes or no. It is simply opening oneself to the possibilities of the moment. What we think we want and what we think we don't want—our hopes and fears— are always what get in the way of our being in the moment.

## OCTOBER 18

I don't have a plan. I am willing for the earth to survive all the forces that threaten to tear it apart, I am willing to let it be as abundant and beautiful as it really is. And I believe there is value in communicating my willingness.

I also believe many of the most powerful prophets (truth-tellers, communicators of the vision) never open their mouths. They transform the world with their presence, simply by having a vision and letting it show in their life, their actions, their interactions, their way of being.

I believe there are people among us—more than a few— who are consciously practicing the silent, invisible transformation of the world around them. This is done by conceiving of a space and allowing it to be filled with love (a visual image is, "surrounding it with white light"). People who practice this act like pumps—like hearts—constantly circulating the energy throughout whatever system they serve, allowing it to return and be renewed and flow out again in a great healing circle.

The technique is not important. What makes a difference is the devotion each one of us has for that portion of the universe that we can see, touch, smell, taste, hear. When we care about what we perceive and are aware of, our caring fills the space around and between the perceived entities, and creates for them an environment of love.

## OCTOBER 19

There is nothing and everything left to say. On odd-numbered days of the month I park on the lefthand side of the street and think my life is empty; on even-numbered days I park on the righthand side and think it full to bursting. Or is it the other way around? The truth is, I have yet to see the pattern; fortunately, that doesn't stop me from seeing the humor.

The pattern of my life is the pattern of my DNA. The things I do are simply a moving picture of who I am. So is my appearance, in fact. Lately I've been noticing more and more that things are what they appear to be. The advice they give secret agents assigned to visit Earth is, "Know that it's an illusion, but always act like it's real." And the only sure way to do this, I suspect, is to practice an ancient yogic discipline called, "taking things at face value."

## OCTOBER 20

Mostly what I see is the face of love. I see it on my children, I see it on my friends, I see it on the woman sleeping next to me now as I write, this extraordinary being who has come to support me and be supported by me for a while, to further her work and mine. We serve the same God.

Some days I see the face of love everywhere, even on me. I see it looking up at me from the fields and streets,

153

looking down at me from the buildings and the sky. And some days of course I think I can't see it at all. And that too is part of the process of being here.

### October 21

When you can't see the face of God, don't search for it. Don't look for love. God and love are everywhere and searching only gets in the way. It's all right not to know. "Seek no contacts and you will find union."

### October 22

Awakening can be so gentle that you don't even know it's happening. And it's okay to let it come easy and it's also okay to have it be dramatic, awesome, overpowering. In fact you can have it both ways, and a thousand others, because this is something we do over and over again. And how nice to live in this world at a time when we're growing aware of the power of breathing and awakening together.

### October 23

After my kids left for school this morning I put on a record and Bob Dylan sang to me. And it suddenly struck me how ready he is to sing to me, from that record, at any time, with no concern for how long it's been or what hour of the day or night. I mean the man's right there. His voice is there. It's a kind of magic.

The truth is we are able to extend ourselves across barriers of space and time. It's kind of cold in my office right now, and so I've got this little heater I can plug in and it will pull electricity from a socket on my wall and run it through some resistance coils so the energy gets slowed down and turns to heat, and then some more of that electricity runs a fan behind the coils that blows the heat in my direction. The juice in my wall comes to me from a wire into my house held

154

up by a rickety relay pole I've come close to bumping into a few times when I park my car. A whole network of wires brings the juice to the pole from dozens or hundreds of miles away where some other kind of power like oil of old fossils or heat in the ground or falling water or wind in mountain passes is translated into this universal and highly communicable form. Zzzooop, I pull the wind from the mountain passes through this little portable heater on my desk and it warms my hands.

And we pretend not to notice these miracles.

And we sit with our thumbs in our mouths and pretend to be powerless and complain about our landlords and all the terrible things that are going on in the world. Or we complain about our tenants. And the weather. And argue about whether God loves us.

## OCTOBER 24

What will it take for enough of us to be willing to give up the luxury of pretending to have no power in this universe? I don't know about you but I chose to come here and chose to have it be exactly the way it is, which reminds me again, I've got to do something about the killings in Guatemala.

## OCTOBER 25

It's painful to be awake, quite often—don't get the illusion that the message is, "Once we wake up, everything will be fine." A lot of people confuse enlightenment with peace. They aspire to a state beyond everyday suffering. But the true bodhisattva is more aware of the suffering in this world than the unawakened person, and commits herself or himself to responding to this suffering and aiding those who are in distress. To perform such work it is not necessary to be free of distress in one's own life; in fact, it is not possible. The work itself brings distress, if one has any feelings, any sensitivity. But I would say that in a real sense it feels better to respond to the distress of other people than to deny that it exists. To respond is to choose life, and I love life. I suppose that means I even love responsibility.

## OCTOBER 26

Of course there are lots of times when I hate responsibility. And an interesting question is, what is the source of this resistance? Often I experience my resistance to responsibility as laziness, you know, "I don't feel like doing what I know I should be doing." And then I wonder why I'm so lazy today (this day and so many other days). But that's the form, or one of the forms, my resistance takes; it sounds almost self-explanatory ("he's just a lazy bum") but in fact calling it laziness doesn't reveal much about the source of my resistance.

(Putting aside the question of source for a moment, I notice that lately I've been having good results by following Christ's advice "I say unto you that ye resist not evil" in relation to my laziness. My normal pattern, built up over three and a half decades, is to push myself harder to "overcome" my desire to do nothing, my desire to avoid whatever it is I think I "should" be doing. And the way I've been improving things for myself a little lately has been by leaning against my normal pattern, by choosing not to resist the evil of laziness, and instead just letting it be there [not necessarily indulging in it, although I do sometimes of course, but not fighting to overcome it either]. And this seems to allow my normal energy flow to reassert itself in time, so that I either do arrive at a place where I can approach that same project without resistance, or else [in time] I come to a moment when I can see there was a certain odd intuitive wisdom in my reluctance, and I'm actually glad I didn't do whatever it was that was so important at the time. In other words, because I'm so used to forcing myself—so used to resisting my own resistance—I now find I can create some space for myself by not resisting, not pushing myself, not letting Time stand over me like a man with a whip, just letting the laziness be there until it passes of its own accord. And it's hard to say for certain, but I have a feeling I'm getting more done than I did when I pushed myself a lot. When I did that, often I ended up doing a lot of busywork which, in retrospect, did nothing to bring me closer to my real goals.)

What is the source of this resistance, of which laziness is one manifestation? I think the source is fear of my own power. I'm afraid of being who I really am. In metaphysical terms, I'm afraid to be God—the one who has power—I'm afraid to be "I AM."

## October 27

And yet all day long I say who I am with every action I take, and so often the force that drives me is to find a way to say it louder. This is the paradox: I'm afraid to know who I am, and I want to tell myself who I am—and these two conditions rule me all day long, they are the source of all my actions and inactions, my activities, my "doing." And all the while I am who I am anyway, and I do it perfectly, at every moment. And that's called, "being."

## October 28

"Being" is not an alternative to "doing." "Doing" is a natural part of "being." What makes a difference is, we have a choice as to where we put our attention.

We can choose to notice what people are doing, or we can choose to see through that and notice who they really are.

We can choose to notice (put our attention on) what we ourselves are doing, or we can choose to see through that, and notice ourselves being who we are.

The latter tends to be the course of forgiveness and love.

## October 29

We are able to extend ourselves across barriers of space and time. Today I got a phone call from Germany. And that's nothing. There are scientists who receive and read messages from millions of years ago. And you don't have to be a professional. No one who visits the Grand Canyon ever fails to receive and be touched by those messages from across the millennia, whether they think of it in those terms or not.

Communication is the great phenomenon of our age, our century. We still think of ourselves as master builders, master adventurers, master organizers, but in a sense those are outdated self-images, more appropriate to the centuries just past. The most striking accomplishments of our contemporary age are all in the realm of communication. Computers don't create information, nor can they be said to be particularly clever in the ways they organize it. What computers are great at is *communicating* information. Airplanes and cars communicate people. Television communicates entertainment (and certain quantities of unasked-for information). Lasers communicate energy.

And what do atomic weapons communicate, if we extend this line of talk to that other familiar contemporary achievement? I believe atomic devices, both weapons and power plants, that use controlled release of thermonuclear energy, are vehicles for communicating power.


## OCTOBER 30

Oddly enough, violations of human rights are also vehicles for communicating power. That's an odd jump, I know, but let's look at it: acts of repression, such as murdering or imprisoning persons who express their opposition to the political status quo (it's happening right now in many if not most nations of the world), are not only used to silence the specific individuals who are killed and jailed. These acts are also means of communicating the power of the state, of those persons who are "in power," so that others will think twice before challenging the state or those who hold office therein. Similarly, acts of terrorism by individuals and groups who are not "in power" are also a way of communicating power. The state says, "we have power"; those who are locked in struggle with the state say, "we are not powerless." And very often we who belong to neither faction are the victims of both.

158

At any rate, I wish to demonstrate that the communication of power plays a tremendous role in our modern world. Its manifestations are everywhere. And all nations that have nuclear weapons would quickly agree that their purpose in having them is to communicate to other nations the power that this nation has (and they would quickly add, "only so those other nations don't get any crazy ideas").

## OCTOBER 31

Nuclear power plants function by releasing (and thus converting to communicable energy, electricity) a power older and more fundamental than that inherent in fossil fuels. Our problem with extending ourselves across these great ranges of space and time (300 million years every time we put gas in our car) is we have some difficulty perceiving the whole picture. Pollution is one consequence of our difficulty in perceiving, and our unwillingness to look at, the whole picture at once.

At present, we are much more able to cope with pollution by hydrocarbons (fossil fuels, some 300,000,000+ years old) than we are with pollution by radiation (atomic fuels, storehouses of an energy that was converted to matter more than five *billion* years ago, according to our current manner of understanding such things). It's probably not entirely a coincidence that we know considerably more of our history for the last three hundred million years than we do of "our" history for the last five billion. We are reaching further back, deeper down, closer to fundament when we work with atomic materials, and that seems to make it harder or more scary for us to see the whole picture.

The bang released by nuclear weapons is also exponentially greater than that released by old-fashioned, hydrocarbon-based weapons. This power we now wave at each other. Is this the ultimate aim of communication, or are we willing to go on from here?

# Chapter Eleven

# NOVEMBER

### NOVEMBER 1

There is a power in each of us that cannot be touched, even by our doubts.

As we become aware of this power, as we begin to acknowledge and respect it, we come to understand that what we "do" is not as important as where we put our attention.

This for me is a real awakening. I have spent most of my life so far absorbed in doing things. And until recently it never occurred to me that the things I do are not the only or even the most important factor determining what I get done.

One example of this is the realization that when I'm with other people, my presence may have more impact on them than anything I say. It is as though there were an invisible power radiating from me. I suppose in the past I could have imagined this being true of certain people, but never myself. I could perhaps imagine that such powers existed, but it would have seemed ridiculous to think of *me* having such power—not someday off in the future but now, and even before now.

If you're like me, you also doubt your own power, and believe that such things are limited to certain very special other people, if they exist at all.

For example: we've all had experiences of the power of physical attraction. An attractive person comes into a room and totally captures your attention. And yet he or she has said and done very little, maybe just indicating by a word or a look that she/he is aware of and could conceivably be interested in your existence—and that's enough, sometimes, to throw your whole life into turmoil. But notice that it was not the word that was said or the little act of flirtation that had the impact on you (imagine the same word or act coming from another person). It was, obviously, the *presence* of that particular man or woman, and the fact that he or she chose, however briefly, to put his or her attention on you.

Sexual attraction is one very common manifestation of the power in us that exists apart from anything we "do." There are many others. Notice how some people can make you laugh or smile without really "doing" anything. Others can make you angry, or make you believe whatever they say, or make you want to take care of them, or make you afraid to look at them. The list goes on forever, and the important thing is not the nature of these powers or the ways they manifest themselves, but rather the simple (and always arguable) observation that these powers are not the result of certain actions—rather the actions arise from the presence of that power, and the tendency for it to take a certain form or forms with this particular person.

The ways we habitually use our personal power, the forms we let it take, are called our "personality." And you, as an observer, may use a person's personality as a clue to

162

their personal power, and to the limitations they place on that power.

But what I wish to emphasize here is this: there is a power in each of us that cannot be touched, not by others, not by ourselves. Our ability to work with, to choose the effects of this power, depends on our willingness to choose where we put our attention.

All the while I've been doing things, I've thought that what I did would determine what I got done. Very often the details of doing have totally absorbed my attention. And when that happens, my attention is *not* on my purpose, on what I want to get done.

Noticing that where I put my attention has more actual impact on things than what I do, has made the world a much bigger and richer place for me. I have a lot more choices, and a lot more willingness to choose.


### NOVEMBER 2

Choose to use your power. Choose to put your attention on what you want, and not on what you don't want. Stay away from denial and false optimism—acknowledge that things are the way they are. Practice these three points, and the results will be extraordinary.


### NOVEMBER 3

Often, of course, the short-term results of conscious and resolute action are not what we might have hoped. Often it takes a lot of faith to go through what we have to go through to get where we're going.

It even takes a lot of faith to go through what we have to go through to be where we are.


### NOVEMBER 4

Everything that comes to me from the universe is a response to something I sent out, consciously or unconsciously,

163

recently or so long ago I pretend I can't remember sending it. Awareness of this is yet another opportunity for me to take responsibility for everything the universe sends my way.

No exceptions! It's all a response to the fact of my being here, and the way I interact with the space around me.

Being rigorous with myself about this awareness is an extraordinary ongoing education for me. I can use it every moment. And I give myself credit for those moments when I actually do use it.

The moments when I don't use it belong to that huge and trivial grouping called "missed opportunities." There are thousands of missed opportunities every hour, and dwelling on even one of them will cause me to miss the next few thousand as well.

The alternative to self-criticism and second-guessing and trying to figure things out is, sitting still. When I sit still, it comes to me . . . and I can feel its natural motion. I love it when I can feel its natural motion. And I always can.

## NOVEMBER 5

If I sit still, it comes to me . . . especially when I'm willing to not know what "it" is. That's the hard part of sitting still: I sit until I think I've got the answer, and then I can't sit still. Impatience masks itself as excitement, I jump up and "it" can't even find me, I'm so busy running around in circles. Next time, can I remember (and be strong enough) to sit still even after I think I have the answer? Time will tell.

## NOVEMBER 6

The one who is wounded and knows he is wounded can be as strong as he is. The one who is wounded and does not know (denies) that he's wounded, cannot be as strong as he is. In believing that self-awareness and self-honesty will weaken us, we deny ourselves.

## NOVEMBER 7

I'm writing about being wounded because I am, this morning. My vulnerability is doubly manifest, in ways that are quite familiar to me: a muscle ache on the side of my neck, a mucus lump in my throat.

It is all right for me to ask why this discomfort, as long as I am willing to admit that I know. It is not necessary or advisable to search for an answer. And if I feel I don't know, the wisest thing is to admit that I'm not willing to admit that I know, and notice that I'm unwilling, and let it go at that.

Do not struggle. And do not struggle not to struggle.

This is not double-talk. This is, I believe, the most direct path out of the discomfort we find ourselves in.

When it is time to take action, we will know. When it is time to wait, we will also know, but sometimes we are impatient. Allow the impatience to be there. And at action time, allow the hesitation, the doubt, the reluctance to be there. Deny no wounds. Be who you are at the moment, and you will find the freedom to be who you are at the moment.

This is not double-talk. This is, I believe, the most direct path out of the discomfort we find ourselves in.


## NOVEMBER 8

The boat approaches the harbor. As our hearts reach out toward shore, let us not forget the final obstacle: fear of completion.

"On the edge of the dream we face our deepest doubts."

The very joy we feel as completion, success, approaches, increases our apprehension that something could go wrong. This apprehension works hand in hand with that part of each of us that is afraid of success because it will increase my responsibilities, catapult me out of the familiar. Fear of failure and fear of success support each other. I whisper in my own ear slanders about how I might abuse my power once I'm sure of it. I urge myself to turn back and I perform little or big acts of sabotage, certain that I cannot handle either the disappointment of failure or the responsibilities of success. The safest course, I tell myself, is to act as though you never intended to complete this crossing in the first place.

After all, there's always next year.

## NOVEMBER 9

If the bridge over the great ocean is completed, we, the human race, will have to walk on it. Are we ready for that? Are we willing?

Are we able to imagine a better world? Or are we pushing and shoving and rushing to build a better world even though we are not yet able to imagine one?

I have no other message than this: allow the vision. And do whatever you must do to bring yourself to a place where you will be able to allow the vision—however long it takes. Start today.

When we can truly allow the vision—when we can imagine a better world, and accept ourselves as worthy of creating it and living in it—everything else will follow.

Do not ask me, or anyone else, for a blueprint. Sit still, and *see* for yourself.

## NOVEMBER 10

The great leap of awareness will not be achieved by the will of a majority triumphing over the resistance of the unawakened. Planetary transformation requires consensus. And a small, modest minority—even a minority of one—can show the way that leads to consensus.

"A few people can build a bridge that can be walked on by many."

Many can lead the way, in different directions, and arrive at the same place.

## November 11

Here's what we can do:
1. create tools
2. make them available
3. set a good example.

## November 12

Above all, what we can do is allow the vision.

## November 13

I need to be alone and I'm afraid or reluctant to be alone. So often the people in my life, particularly women I love and am close to, get caught in the middle of this little conflict I'm having with myself, and it must seem to them like they can't do anything right, I don't want them around and I won't allow them to leave.

I can get pretty nasty about it too. The most serious conflicts are the ones we have with ourselves. I can forgive you for anything. But I'll chew you up if you get in the way of my unwillingness to forgive myself.

Right now, for example, I need to be alone. But that's challenging, and so when my lady invites me to be with her, I'm tempted. I want to use her as a place to hide. And also I don't want to hide, I want to complete what I'm doing. I'm frustrated with my own ability to be tempted, my weakness. And I find myself directing my anger at her.

You know how when two people are fighting, they can both turn to fight off the outsider who tries to interfere and make peace? That's what happens when you interrupt my struggles with myself: both sides of me turn and start shouting at you.

## NOVEMBER 14

Falling in love takes us outside of ourselves for a while. And then it flips, and puts us face to face with ourselves more than we ever were before. That's when things start getting difficult between men and women. We want to hide in the arms of the very person whose presence is awakening us, and it doesn't work.

## NOVEMBER 15

Being loved puts me in touch with my power, with who I really am. It brings me great joy. And at the same time it scares me. I think I'm scared of losing all this joy, but that's not the worst part. What really scares me is being aware of my power. I don't feel ready to handle being who I really am.

Being loved puts me face to face with what I've been running away from all my life.

## NOVEMBER 16

Success does the same thing. It takes us outside of ourselves, and then it confronts us with ourselves. It brings great joy and great fear. It gives us the freedom we want and also forces on us the responsibility we've been avoiding.

Each one of us is pursued by God. We chase success and love, and flee from personal responsibility and self-knowledge. We run in circles.

And the closer we get, the faster we run away.

## NOVEMBER 17

Do I love her, or do I love the way she loves me? I do love the way she loves me, that much is certain, and I notice that the idea that she might stop loving me makes me nervous. And it's all right, too. The last woman taught me I'm good-looking. (Wasn't easy!) This one has taught me that I'm lovable, and she's done a good job of it. She's taught me so well, and I'm enjoying being loved so much, I'm not even afraid of what the future might bring.

It sure means a lot to me, that I'm finally willing and able and happy to be the object instead of the subject. Not that one's better than the other. It's just nice to make a change sometimes.

## NOVEMBER 18

I'm willing to be loved. There was a time when I couldn't say that, and a time when I said it but didn't mean it the way I mean it now. And no doubt there's still plenty of room for expansion. I was so closed for so long, and I'm just starting to open my arms.

And am I willing to love at the same time? I don't know. I always have been, always been a fool for love, I'm so used to it I can't even trust it, don't know if it's really me or just an overly-familiar self-image. Who I think I am. Am I willing to love? Yes, I am. Just a little, maybe, but enough. I'm willing to love without using love as a protection against being loved, and that's a big step for me.

## NOVEMBER 19

I'm willing to take the next step. And that's all one has to do in this world. It may be a very small step, but the willingness to take it is the willingness to keep going, and that's our salvation, and the source of all future creation. The apostles said to Jesus, "Increase our faith." (Luke 17:6) And Jesus said, "If you had faith as a grain of mustard seed, you might say to this sycamine tree, be plucked up by the root and planted in the sea, and it would obey you." In other words, Jesus said if you have any faith at all, you have enough. Use it, and there is no limit to your power.

## November 20

It's true that there tend to be tremendous limits on our willingness to use our power. That's why the willingness to take the next step, however small, is the key to transformation. And when we are willing to act without being assured of the outcome, with no secure knowledge of what lies ahead or whether we can handle it, when we are willing to step into darkness, that is called faith.

Just getting up in the morning requires faith. Choosing to bring a child into the world takes a lot of faith. Each one of us, no matter how great our doubts, no matter how fiercely we protect ourselves against disappointment, still has a mustard seed of faith.

## November 21

Use it. Take the next step.

## November 22

Do not deny your knowledge. It is a great servant, and deserves your devotion and respect. But if you should ever find yourself in a place where you must momentarily choose between knowledge and faith, remember which is the more solid of the two.

Every one of us has leaned on knowledge and had it fail us, at one time or another. But faith, by definition, can never fail us, for to have faith is to choose to accept the consequences.

## November 23

When I look at my own words, I am appalled at how easily they can be misunderstood. A friend of mine woke up one morning to find that her daughter and her friend's daughter had thrown a shirt over a light bulb the previous night, to hide the fact that the light was on. When the mothers came in in the morning the shirt was smoldering, ready to burst into flames. My friend told her friend not to be upset, that if there were any true danger they would have been warned somehow, intuition would have made them check on their daughters in time. She "knows" this to be so. And she, and you and I, could read the words I wrote above and believe this to be a perfect example of leaning on faith instead of knowledge.

No, no, no, no, no! I've failed, you see. And how many little girls must burn up in the night because my carelessness with words has encouraged their parents to go on being unconscious (and to advise their friends to be unconscious, in order to assuage their own guilt)?

My impulse on the one hand is to tear up the book, rather than risk being responsible for such misunderstandings, and the disasters they bring. (How many fools "have faith" that they can drive home carefully and safely even though they've had a few drinks.

But this is exactly the point. I could back off, I could tear up my book, and withhold whatever it might have to offer, or simply back up a few sections and withhold my remarks on faith, and pretend that that's enough. Or I could take the next step.

That's what I'm doing. I'm not denying my knowledge. I know that what I wrote can easily be misinterpreted, with horrible consequences. And I choose to acknowledge that this is real, and that in a sense the whole book has led up to this moment, so it does no good to back up a few pages. This has been the next step, to acknowledge this, to let my own discomfort serve to call attention to the problem. And the next step now is to find a way to clear up the misunderstanding.


## November 24

(I don't like having my whole book, this year of effort, rest on my ability to clarify this always murky issue of real faith versus self-deception. But you know, in a real sense the worth of everything we've done in our whole lives until now

171

always rests on our actions at this moment. This fact comforts the sinner and terrifies the righteous, but in any event it will always be true that everything rests on right action at this moment.)

(If this terrifies you, as it does me, let me remind you again to breathe. Breathe out as well as in. "No inspiration without expiration," that's our motto. It also means that good deeds and brilliant ideas must not be written in stone.)

NOVEMBER 25

Tests for "faith":

*Must* I choose between knowledge and faith in this situation? (In the case of the smoldering shirt, certainly not. Knowledge tells us that something has happened that one does not wish to happen again, and that attention to this can turn the incident into an opportunity: i.e., a sobering reminder of the need to educate even young children in possible fire hazards . . . and an opportunity to notice the potential usefulness of smoke alarms. Realization that you actually could have lost your children, or your house, is unpleasant and therefore useful, potentially cutting through the procrastination that keeps us from getting around to teaching our kids and installing safety devices, replacing "just another day" with a sense of urgency. . . . But even if knowledge were not so obviously beneficial, or not beneficial at all, the test is still valid: *must* you choose? Are knowledge and faith absolutely in conflict here? No. You can have faith that your children are protected by your love and God's love, and still act on what your knowledge tells you, which is that this is an unacceptable situation and you need to do something about it if you can. There's room for both, even when the knowledge is frustrating and you can't find an appropriate response, a way to prevent a recurrence. And in the case at hand, as in so many others, knowledge and faith work together—your knowledgeable response to the situation allows you to be God's instrument, actively working to make your faith a reality.)

Is it self-serving? (This test for faith must be rigorously

applied. Ultimately a "yes" answer does not necessarily mean that this is not a case of "real faith." But the process of examining the situation to discover whether what we're calling "faith" is actually self-serving can be very revealing. If one is rigorous here, one tends to "catch oneself in the act," shattering the illusion that the choice you're making is a righteous one. In the case of the smoldering shirt, my friend's faith in her and her friend's intuition is obviously self-serving: she is trying to tell her friend that there was no real danger, so that she herself doesn't have to feel guilty, or confront her own failings. This is called denial. There is a better way to handle this: to acknowledge that one is responsible, and then to choose consciously not to indulge in guilt, but to learn from the situation instead, so that insofar as possible it will not be repeated, and other related dangers can be avoided as well. . . . Remember, the "is it self-serving?" test cannot be satisfied with a simple yes or no. Its effectiveness lies in the process of rigorous self-examination it sets in motion—a process in which guilt, righteousness, defensiveness, etc. should be excluded, put aside, as much as possible. That's part of what makes it rigorous. Ask yourself, "How do I benefit from believing this is a matter of faith?" If performed with good intent, this question will awaken you.)

Am I willing to accept the consequences? (This is the really hard question, and it must be asked. Faith means a willingness to accept the consequences, whatever they are, and with the awareness that we cannot know what the consequences will be. I trust that if my friend had asked herself this question, her glibness would have dissolved in an instant. How many of us would say, "Yes, I'm willing to accept the consequences, in this case the possible death of my daughter, if it turns out I'm wrong about what I 'know' to be so"? Faith comes when we know we've done our part, and we're willing to surrender to the will of God. Faith must never be an excuse for not doing our part. Like, I get scared before taking a long trip by plane or boat. I could put my energy into denying that there's any danger—which takes a lot of energy, since in fact there is some danger always. Or I can acknowledge my fear, and ask, "Is this trip necessary?" I search my soul, as it were. And if I find that the trip really is necessary, then my experience is I am more willing to expose myself to danger. Not because I'm "sure" God won't let me die if I'm doing the right thing, but more along the lines of, if I do die, no matter how remote the possibility, let it be while I was acting consciously and on purpose and not unconsciously. The possibility of death helps keep us awake and in the moment.)

Is what I call "faith" actually a form of denial? (Of course we wish to deny the possibility of death, or anything bad, ever happening to ourselves or our loved ones. Unfortunately, such denial—refusal to wear seat belts while driving around the neighborhood—greatly increases that possibility. But we have to be willing to admit we're not perfect, and that the urge to deny comes up again and again in all of us, if we're to apply this test with any effectiveness. Again, it must be applied rigorously. If it is, it provides us with excellent opportunities to "catch ourselves in the act." The application of this test to the case of the smoldering shirt should be obvious. If it isn't, read this whole section again. In fact, read it again anyway. Thank you.)

### NOVEMBER 26

I said a while back that there is no blueprint. I was talking about planetary awakening, but of course it applies to personal transformation as well. In writing what I write in these pages I am not attempting to provide you with answers, though I suppose it must seem like that sometimes. The most I can actually do is acquaint you with a way of thinking.

A great deal of the time what we call faith is really laziness or self-deception. We expect God to do for us what we won't do for ourselves. My intention is not to condemn this attitude (though I know I can get quite snotty about it), but rather to demonstrate that it doesn't serve us. God is more than willing to do Her part, but that doesn't help us unless we're willing to do our part at the same time. And doing our part is demanding, rigorous: it requires us to do what is most difficult for us, which is to acknowledge and use our own power.

God set us up to flunk out of the Garden of Eden (and obviously He or She did set it up; He/She knew perfectly well our weakness) because He *wanted* us to have knowledge, He wanted us to start moving towards taking our share of the responsibility. He wants us to be as Gods, because He has other things to do and isn't interested in wiping our asses for all eternity. And She/He set it up the way She did because She wanted us to choose. We knew the choice: we could be obedient and stay in the garden, or we could eat the fruit of the tree of knowledge of good and evil, and be on our own. We chose freedom; we chose responsibility; and at that moment God was a proud parent, no matter what the legend tells you. And we are still trying to live up to that choice. And I suppose we are still trying to avoid its consequences, as well.

There are moments when we do have to choose between leaning on knowledge and leaning on faith. They are the moments when we must decide to take the next step, even though we don't *know* what the outcome will be. That is the time for real faith. And when you lean on that faith, you will find it to be the solid rock that knowledge can never be, because knowledge only goes as far as where we've ever been ... and faith goes one step further.


### NOVEMBER 27

Adam and Eve got us started on this, they Fell and we're still Falling. They chose to dive into the unknown, and gave up the ultimate security to do so. And I for one am glad. Even in the face of atomic holocaust, I think they made the right choice. Nor would I go back and uneat the apple of knowledge of atomic energy. The challenge for us is to go forward from here. And I have faith that we can handle it.


### NOVEMBER 28

The way of thinking presented in this book is a way of thinking you're already comfortable with, or you couldn't

175

have read this far. So I'm offering nothing new. What this really is is a workbook, an opportunity to exercise your way of thinking, a companion to practice with, a friend. I don't see myself as a purveyor of new ideas. I see myself as someone with the unmitigated gall to write down and publish the obvious. And I see you as someone modest enough and wise enough to be willing to be reminded of the obvious. I honor you. When enough of us remember enough of what we already know enough of the time, we will all be unable to keep our eyes closed. And, according to the ancient legend, we'll all wake up together.

### NOVEMBER 29

What this really is is a place for me to play. I hope you're enjoying it too.

### NOVEMBER 30

Thank you for being my companion. Sitting still and taking the next step can both get lonely sometimes.

## Chapter Twelve

# DECEMBER

### DECEMBER 1

Almost anything can happen today, no matter what day today happens to be. Time is something very elastic, subjective. Human beings laugh at the dinosaurs for dying out, we say they were stupid. But human beings haven't been around a tenth as long as the dinosaurs were.

Some people like to tell us what is and isn't important. They want us to look at what matters in the long run. Maybe in the long run a thousand years for us is a weekend for some other creature. Maybe in the long run beings from another universe planted human beings in the earthly ecology a couple of million years ago, and they're taking bets on whether we'll survive as long as the dinosaurs did.

The bettors naturally divide into two cheering sections: those who bet on us, and want us to make it, because they have money riding on this; and those who bet against us, and want us to fail, maybe because they feel sentimental about the dinosaurs. If the rules of the game allow interference with the playing conditions (or if the bettors aren't above cheating a little) this would explain the widely-held theory that there are angels and devils struggling with each other to influence our daily actions.

### DECEMBER 2

Now let's go a little further with this science fiction scenario. Suppose that there's a side bet that's developed in the last few thousand years, in which one group of bettors (they claim to be scientists, conducting experiments, just like stock market gamblers pretend to be interested in business) says that humans have a tremendous advantage over the dinosaurs because of their ability to acquire knowledge, and another group says that this is in fact the humans' greatest liability. They say that knowledge will cause humans to destroy themselves long before natural forces would have got them, long before they can begin to catch up with the dinosaurs' record (the d's held out for roughly a hundred million earth years).

There's excitement in the betting room: the human ability to acquire and communicate knowledge has been accelerating at a rapid pace in the last few hundred years, and now a conceptual breakthrough has taken place as humans have learned to unleash, in a rather crude way, the power locked up in atoms, the basic building blocks of their universe.

To many observers it seems obvious that such frenzied activity can only end in extraordinary disorder, that now that humans have knowledge of how to blow apart their own planet they are certain to do exactly that. What's to stop them? Common sense? Respect for what God has created? Hah! says group A. Humans may be smart enough to design and build these weapons, but no way are they smart enough to not use them.

Group B is a little worried at this turn of events, to tell the truth, but the true believers among the pro-human, pro-knowledge group are enthusiastic. They say that this rapid acceleration of knowledge and communication-ability is the unmistakable climax stage of the evolution in consciousness that will allow humans to adapt to and even influence earthly and celestial events, ultimately allowing them a longevity far beyond that of the dinosaurs. They say that as humans awaken into an awareness of who and what they've become, they'll be able to deal with this nuclear self-destruct problem relatively easily.

This is called the "awakening" theory. The skeptics say, "Look at human history! They've never learned any self-control. And it's always been brother against brother." The believers say, "This human history you speak of is only the last six thousand years, and these creatures have been around for a million or two. The process of rapid acquisition of knowledge has distorted their values, no question about it; but as they awaken they will also remember the peaceful, modest ways that allowed them to live on this planet for so long already. And at the same time they will awaken with an ability to work together and influence natural events in their universe that was hardly imagined by their forebears."

"*If* they make it." "They've already made it."

The arguments continue into the night, not in a hostile tone but with the good-hearted jostling that goes on among long-time companions. When this bet is resolved or they get bored with it and lose interest, they'll move on to something else.

### December 3

Meanwhile we humans don't have the luxury of knowing whether this scenario is true or not—for that matter, if it were true, we still wouldn't know which side was right. So if we care about our own survival, we must assume the greatest possible danger, and respond appropriately. Now is the time to use our knowledge, and any other tricks we've acquired along the way. Faith and love are two that come to mind.

### DECEMBER 4

Let nothing stand in the way of our ability to feel and express love, our ability to lean on our faith in the forces that we have always known and that interact with us at each moment, and our ability to learn and to use our knowledge in our own behalf.

And let us know that in fact nothing does stop us from using these abilities we have, as long as we choose to believe this is so; that is, as long as we choose life.

And now put your hands on me and speak to me in the language that is apart from and beyond all words. Touch and let yourself be touched. Heal and be healed.

### DECEMBER 5

Lovers as always have the job of assuring the preservation and continuation of the species. Lovers become parents. And lovers and parents are the humans who care the most about other human beings.

### DECEMBER 6

And some don't care. And some who are neither lovers nor parents do care. It's the caring that's important, not the category you're in.

### DECEMBER 7

What is important now is our intention.

Notice where you put your attention. That on which you put your attention is called your intention.

It's not what you say you want. It's where your attention is that makes the difference.


### DECEMBER 8

Almost anything can happen today. And time is not a limitation. When we choose our limits, we use time as an excuse, among other excuses. And when we forget all that, we find ourselves in the midnight hour.


### DECEMBER 9

The great opportunity that has been given us is that we are alive today. If we wish to complain about the state of the world or the circumstances of our personal lives, we must first find a way to forget this extraordinary gift we've been given. To forget, we must dim our awareness. In doing so, we lose touch with God, with ourselves, with the miracle of being here and the power we have as a result of being here. We choose to go to sleep, we choose to see ourselves as powerless.

And yet every one of us is, equally, a fulcrum from which the world can be moved. The only limits on our power are the ones we choose to put on it. "Argue for your limitations and they are yours." Anything can happen today. And since we're here, you or I can exert tremendous influence on what does happen, by using our power in any of ten thousand ways. What makes the difference is where we choose to put our attention.

The less attention we put on our own alleged powerlessness, the more powerful and effective our intention becomes, without our actually "doing" anything. All we have to do is notice that we're here, and what's going on around us and inside us. This is called being awake in the moment.


### DECEMBER 10

The midnight hour is for celebration. Friendship, sex, music, appreciation of nature are pleasures of the midnight hour. We get caught up in the energy of it all and forget about the past and the future. And awaken refreshed. Sometimes the universe catches us and embraces us and lets us rediscover its newness.

### December 11

Being in the moment is a natural function, an innate ability, like breathing, that can be enhanced by conscious application.

If you notice you're out of the moment (your attention is somewhere else), don't dwell on it. Let go, lightly. If there's something you can't let go of, notice that, and just be with it (without thinking about it). Don't try to get back to a particular moment, any more than you try to breathe a particular mouthful of air. Choose to be here and now.

### December 12

And when the whole idea of "being here" becomes oppressive, an effort, dig a pit and bury these words and concepts ten feet deep and never think about them again. You don't need them. You already know. You already are.

### December 13

Men and women is a subject that never bores me, never gets old, because no matter how much I think I've learned, it's never enough to get me through the next five minutes. As my awareness grows, the mystery deepens. The more I know, the further I go, and the further I go, the more I discover that I don't know. And constantly I am brought up against my own blindness. That's not surprising. What is surprising is how often male/female attraction inspires me to go over or around my own barriers. Motivation. She moves me. Nothing else can move me quite so irrationally or relentlessly. I acknowledge her power. And it isn't her, or me. It's both of us, and something else. I don't know the name of this force, but I know from personal experience that this is what sets the universe in motion, over and over again.


## DECEMBER 14

There is nothing more sexy than a pretty face. Why? Is this a conditioned response, are we looking for archetypes? That's not my experience. None of the women I've known in my life have looked like each other. So what do I see, when I see beauty? I think it's something so personal that it's not only unique to my eyes, it's unique to my eyes when I'm looking at you. I mean, other people don't see what I see, and I don't even see it except when I'm looking at your face.

There's a leap my heart takes when I see something that looks pretty to me. And I do see beauty everywhere. So my experiences of beauty are connected for me by the way it feels, the excitement. I can look at different faces and have relatively similar experiences. But the content of what I see is never the same, that to me is the mystery. What is it I'm seeing each time? The best I can do is say that I'm recognizing a part of me, or a part of what I love in the world, in each person I'm attracted to, and every time it's a different part. I am large, I contain multitudes. And your beauty, what I see in your face, somehow puts me in touch with a part of the universe that is very important to me. It awakens parts of me I'd forgotten I missed. It's as though the first time I see you, I remember all the moments we will have spent together before our lives are over. My longing for you is a memory of the future.


## DECEMBER 15

We chose to come here to experience being human. What have we got to complain about? Have we been deprived of that experience? Is there anyone out there who's been cheated out of his or her appropriate portion of pain or joy? What I want you to know is that the club isn't closed, regardless of what it says on the door. Just walk on in as if you owned the place. You do. You're the one we've been waiting for. The dancing will continue till morning.

## DECEMBER 16

Informed optimism means being aware of how bad things are, and how good things are, and then using this information as the foundation of a positive vision of where we can go from here if we so choose (if we choose to do the work) (if we choose to allow the vision).

Uninformed optimism is the same as denial, it's a refusal to be aware (paradoxically, we refuse to open our eyes because we already know what we'd see that we're afraid of seeing; so we already are aware of what we refuse to be aware of; so we acknowledge that we know in the very act of denial). All denial does is slows things down. But that's okay, you go ahead and deny, we'll hold the boat until you're ready. We'll even let you shout and holler and create a disturbance to prevent someone else from blurting out the truth. Acknowledging that you're part of us and letting you go through whatever you have to go through to be here right now is the shortest possible path to our mutual awakening. If the rest of us awaken and just pretend that you're with us, we'll only have to go through the whole thing over again.

## DECEMBER 17

I'm sitting in my office. When we moved into this house almost eight years ago, there was a garage full of junk out back. My brother helped me remove the junk, and it's been my office ever since. Much of this book has been written out here. The garage door swings open on summer days. Now it's cold and rainy and the heater's on. The telephone has an answering machine and there's a clock to remind me how close it's getting to mail-time. Mail goes out of this small town once a day, and I notice the main pressure I place on myself each day is this feeling that I've got to get it done by mail-time. After mail-time passes I relax, whether I've got "it" done or not. The next deadline won't be till tomorrow.

## DECEMBER 18

*Common Sense* says we're here to take action and have an effect on the world. I believe this, and I advocate it. I advocate it indiscriminately; that is, I even urge people I don't like and who disagree with me to act and let their power, their influence, be felt. I don't do this to be fair; I do this because I think it works out best for everyone this way. The hope of humankind, and of all the other creatures and forms of life whose destiny is linked with that of humankind, is for us to function as a conscious, self-sustaining ecological unit in the universe, and for success at this (survival on an ongoing basis) to be our intention, our primary goal. I have no doubt that if we again make survival our primary goal (as we did for so many millennia, collectively as well as individually), we'll make it.

And I believe the form of our conscious, self-sustaining ecological unit cannot be imposed from without. It doesn't matter whether what one tries to impose is benevolent or malevolent, and it doesn't matter whether one tries to impose it by reason or by force (anyway reason has a funny tendency to make use of force when it's not getting the respect it thinks it deserves). Our experience tells us that what is imposed from without does not hold together. It isn't self-sustaining. And after a while it's always a direct insult to consciousness.

Ideas and institutions get old, in other words. And in the struggles that accompany the imposition (and expiration) of ideas and institutions, we inevitably lose sight of what we really want, what's really important to us: our daily lives, our individual and collective existence, and the content thereof.

So I believe the form of our conscious, self-sustaining ecological unit, humankind, the biosphere, must be expressed from within. And what that looks like in my imagination is four billion humans (and umpteen billion other living organisms) each acting out their own individual DNA, or sense of what's right. So I urge every one of us to take action and have

185

an effect on the world, because I think this is how the collective organism functions. The organism as a whole is healthy when each cell is healthy and performing its particular role. (And we don't have to know what our roles are to perform them. We've been doing it all our lives. Indeed, if we want to know what our roles are, we might look at what we've been doing all our lives. And if that look causes us to alter our activities in some way, that's perfect too.)

If this sounds like a call for unrestricted individualism, I might add that many individuals will have the impulse to join with others to work together on something that feels right to all of them. And these groups can work with other groups. As long as the sense of purpose tends to travel from the bottom up rather than the top down, our conscious ecological unit has an excellent chance of surviving.

### DECEMBER 19

So I'm not saying we should "do" something. I'm saying that we are doing things all day long, and since we are, we can have an incredible impact by making the extra effort of paying attention to what we do, and choosing to do what we feel is right. You may say we're doing this already. But I notice that we're not, a lot of the time, and we're not because we believe that what we do doesn't make a difference. We don't believe in our own power.

### DECEMBER 20

It does make a difference.

### DECEMBER 21

And the one last thing I need to say about this is that the word "survival" suggests an unhappy, bare-bones, no-frills existence, suggests that even freedom gets the backseat to just making it through; it sounds unromantic, ignoble, low.

186

It sounds like we have to put the finer things of life aside, like sex and creativity, conversation, good food, friendship, and just concentrate on minimal necessities. And yet you know from reading this book that that's not what I believe in at all. If the revolution (or the evolution)'s not going to be fun, I say the hell with it.

The point is that the finer things in our lives, whatever they are, are the absolutely essential ingredient in collective survival, because these things, these aspects of our experience, the midnight hour and all that other good stuff, are what *motivate* us, much more than logic or even hunger ever could. "Survival" means "living on," and these aspects of our lives inspire us and motivate us to go on living, whatever it takes. This is what winds us up and gets the planetary organism moving, at the lowest, most basic level: the pleasure each of us finds in saying to the world, one way or another, "I am."


### DECEMBER 22

Art, sex, conversation, good food, gardening, friendship are a few of the ten thousand ways of saying to the universe, "I am."

Practice the ten thousand ways, and you are fulfilling your purpose. And if you pay attention, you might notice the universe saying back to you, with a smile, "you are."


### DECEMBER 23

I am alive. I love being alive, and I love it in a way that makes me realize it's not appropriate to think of life and death as opposites. The rabbit runs fast, and loves to run fast; but the rabbit wouldn't need to run, and would never even have developed the ability, if there were no fox, if there were no deadly pursuer. Even the rabbit's sexual appetite is a function of its vulnerability. The fecundity of the species is a response to the permanent danger that is a rabbit's life, a response to the standing emergency.

Sometimes when we say we want peace we mean we

want sleep, rest, lack of stimulus, death. Exhausted by struggling against fear and uncertainty, we believe the only alternative to the struggle is defeat. But Christ teaches us, and the *I Ching* teaches us, and all great teachers must go on teaching us, that it is wise not to struggle, even against evil ... and that by not-struggling while continuing to bear in mind what we know to be right we plant the seeds of ultimate victory.

Peace does not mean the absence of war. I don't believe we want a world without conflict, any more than we want friendships or love relationships in which there is no conflict. The rabbit does not really want a world in which there is no need to run or raise large families, in which there is no purpose in being built like a rabbit.

Peace is a temporary absence of agitation. In terms of the nuclear issue, when we say we want peace we mean we want to believe again that our children's children will have a planet to live on. We are not saying we want an end to all danger, but rather that we want a danger we can live with, not a danger so horrible that we must block our awareness of it at every moment or else go mad.

This sort of peace is within our reach. It requires a willingness to know how bad things are, in terms of the physical danger we have created, and how good things are, in terms of the intelligence and adaptability of humans as individuals and as a species. We must believe that humans can set a goal and achieve it. And then we must be willing to set an appropriate goal.

Our goal, I think, is agreement. We need to achieve consensus, unanimous agreement, that we want to go on living, that we want to continue the human experiment, and that there are no conditions on this—i.e., terms which, if they are not met, would cause us to renounce the agreement.

I am not talking about something that "looks like" agreement: you know, your representative and my representative get together and sign a sheet of paper. I am talking about real agreement, real consensus. If you want to ask about enforcement, then I have not yet communicated the essence of what I'm suggesting ... because true consensus requires no enforcement. It easily and naturally enforces itself.

We ask too much if we ask an end to all danger, or an

188

end to all suffering; indeed, we ask for something we don't really want. That sort of paradox sets our power against itself.

The essence of what I'm suggesting is that we reach consciously for the minimum possible agreement that can unite us all: the agreement that we are willing to be here and to acknowledge that nothing is more important than going on with the show.

If successful, we would then, in this one matter of the will to survive, become a conscious being, united in a single intention, all of our power working together to achieve the daily miracle of continued survival. You can't just do this once and forget about it. But I have confidence that once we've experienced the power of human agreement we'll find ourselves choosing life again and again.

## DECEMBER 24

Indeed, it is not inconceivable to me that this agreement has already been reached, and that all that remains is to become conscious of it. This possibility however, that we have already reached agreement and are already using our collective power to avoid species and planetary death, must not become a source of complacency. We can no more afford complacency than the rabbit can. We are vulnerable, and the truth is we have chosen to be vulnerable, we love being vulnerable, we love this temporary existence. It is demanding, and we like to have demands made of us. We like to be awake.

## DECEMBER 25

Sometimes we set up a false choice between freedom and survival. It is true that survival of the spirit is the most important thing, and when your spirit is threatened you'll know it, and will face death gladly if need be to protect it. But it is unwise and unnecessary to anticipate such a situation, for it takes place in a realm outside of and unrelated to intellectual awareness.

189

To proclaim that an intellectual concept of freedom is more important than species survival may seem noble, but it is based on a misunderstanding. Human freedom does not exist in the absence of humans. If our choice were (and it is not) species extinction or two thousand years of tyranny, faith in God and in ourselves would require that we choose the tyranny. To resist evil is to join it and strengthen it. Destroying the human race in the name of fighting for freedom is the ultimate example of the folly of confronting evil with its own weapons.

A person may die for his family, his country, his beliefs. It is implicit in our romanticizing of such heroism that others survive to benefit in some way from his courage. But what may a species die for? Who benefits—especially when that species takes most of the biosphere with it when it goes?

We must agree to survive, and then we can spend all eternity if we wish staying true to and perfecting the ideal of human freedom. This is not cowardice but the most profound form of courage, the courage to endure.

## DECEMBER 26

The choice we face as a species is not so overwhelming when we realize it is the same choice we face as individuals every day: the choice to get out of bed in the morning and go on with the business of living.

## DECEMBER 27

What you or I can contribute is our willingness to find ourselves in agreement with all humans everywhere. I don't think it even matters what we agree on. The important thing is to look and see whether we're willing to have this experience. For each of us there will probably be some rough spots, some points of resistance ("I don't want to be in agreement with *them*!"). Be patient with yourself. Work on your resistance gently, or just let it be. Your desire to arrive at willingness is enough. No one knows how long this process will take. What we can do is begin.

### DECEMBER 28

The thing to do is take the next breath. And every breath is a new beginning.

### DECEMBER 29

We make love, we fall asleep together, later we wake up together. And while we sleep, side by side or in each other's arms, is it not possible that we dream together?

Perhaps we don't know as much as we think we do about lovemaking and its consequences. Maybe, for example, genetic patterns exist as much in our electromagnetic auras as in our cells; maybe two auras come into contact and build a bridge across which information travels (just as in biological sex), sometimes resulting in the creation of an energy descended from but independent of the parent energies. And this has been going on all along, millions of years, but we haven't noticed it lately because we're putting so much attention on each other's bodies (and well worth the attention, they are).

I like the idea that we humans are here not only to live together but to dream together. And just as we live not only with other humans but with the air, the microscopic creatures, plants, animals, all living things, so also we dream not only with each other but side by side with the trees, the birds, house pets, microbes, even rocks. We dream on and with the Earth, and with all creatures of the Earth, and maybe with heavenly creatures as well. We are part of a web of consciousness just as we are part of the great chain of being. We are linked, and our linking is not passive but active.

### DECEMBER 30

I have to laugh at myself, thinking out loud like this, just as if I wasn't one page away from the end of the book

I've been working on all year. The truth is, we only stop coming up with new ideas because we tell ourselves, that's it, no more new ideas now, I'm full up. And we stop and try to make sense of it all. But it doesn't work. You can't make sense of anything when you stop. To see the patterns as they are, you have to keep moving with them.

### DECEMBER 31

Almost anything can happen on this page, or this planet. Thank you for creating with me.

# INDEX

This index is incomplete; it is meant to be helpful rather than thorough. Following the index are blank pages for your own index notes—a place to write down dates and subjects of passages you may want to find again.

# PERSONAL INDEX

# PERSONAL INDEX

# PERSONAL INDEX

# PERSONAL INDEX

# BIOGRAPHICAL NOTE

Paul Williams is an author and "practical philosopher" whose activities have included writing a much-loved, best-selling handbook for conscious living; starting the first American rock music magazine; living in an idealistic commune in the Canadian wilderness; editing the first book edition of the International Bill of Rights; leading personal growth workshops in the United States and Europe; and serving for more than eight years as a small town volunteer fireman. He says his common purpose in all these activities has been to encourage people to appreciate and use their own power.

Williams was born in May, 1948 and founded *Crawdaddy*, "The Magazine of Rock," in 1966. His books include *Outlaw Blues* (on rock music); *Das Energi* (an awareness handbook that has touched more than a million people since its publication in 1973); *Apple Bay; Coming; The Book of Houses* (a breakthrough work on personal growth cycles, with astrologer Robert Cole); *Dylan—What Happened?; Common Sense;* and (as editor) *The International Bill of Human Rights*. Williams is publisher of Entwhistle Books and was recently named literary executor for American novelist and science fiction writer Philip K. Dick.

Williams lives with his two sons in a small house in northern California.

Typeset in Aldine Roman by Richard Ellington, Oakland, California. Printed and bound on the Cameron Book System by Kingsport Press, Kingsport, Tennessee. Dust jacket printed at Superior Press, Oakland, California. Additional camera work by Design Enterprises, Berkeley, California. Cover airbrush by Planet Remodeling, Daly City, California.

# THE INTERNATIONAL BILL OF HUMAN RIGHTS

The basic rights of all human beings have been written down and agreed to in a document called "The International Bill of Human Rights." (The 1983 Planetary Initiative Congress called this Bill "probably the most noble achievement of the 20th Century.") This process began in 1948 at the United Nations, and climaxed in 1976 when the Bill was ratified by enough nations to take on the force of international law.

This is the beginning. The next step is for this Bill to become as much a part of international consciousness as the American Bill of Rights is in the U.S.

In 1981 Paul Williams discovered that one reason so few people know about the International Bill is that it had never been available in book form. He remedied this by editing and publishing an inexpensive book edition of the Bill, with introductions by Nobel Peace Prize winner Adolfo Pérez Esquivel and former U.S. president Jimmy Carter.

Williams also helped found THYB, a nonprofit corporation dedicated to human rights education. Since 1981, THYB has distributed the book edition of the Bill to thousands of schools and libraries. (The name THYB is from a Japanese phrase meaning "the bridge over the great ocean.")

Copies of the International Bill can be ordered with the coupon on the last page of this book. The prices are:     paperback, $3.25     hardcover, $9.95 Make checks to Entwhistle Books and include $1 postage per order.

If you would like to take part in the campaign to make the International Bill of Human Rights known to all the people of the world, please consider making a tax-deductible contribution to THYB with the coupon below. Every dollar you send to THYB allows us to donate a free copy of the book edition of the International Bill to a school or library. If you wish, you can specify the school(s) or library you want the books donated to.

Send the coupon to THYB, Box 574, Glen Ellen, CA 95442, or you can enclose your THYB check and coupon with any order you send to Entwhistle Books. Or write to the THYB Human Rights Project for more information.

- - - - - - - - - - - - - - - - - - - - - - - - - - - - - - - - - -

Enclosed please find $_____ as a tax-deductible donation to THYB. I understand that for every dollar I enclose, one copy of **The International Bill of Human Rights** will be given to a school or library.

Name_____

Address_____

_____ Zip_____

[Your name and address are for our records. No donation is too small. If you would like to specify a school, school district, church, or library that you would like to receive a copy or copies of the Bill, write the name(s) and address(es) on the back of this coupon. This coupon may be Xeroxed, cut out, or you can put the information on a plain sheet of paper.]

Send to/checks payable to: **THYB, Box 574, Glen Ellen, CA 95442**

additional copies of

**WAKING UP TOGETHER**

may be ordered from:      Entwhistle Books
                        Box 611
                        Glen Ellen, CA 95442

1 copy:      $12.50

2 copies:    $22.50

3 copies:    $32.50

special:     10 copies, $90.00

Make checks payable to Entwhistle Books.

Xerox or cut out coupon on next page, or write name & address, books ordered and amount enclosed on a sheet of paper. Add tax and shipping as indicated on coupon.

◇ ◇ ◇ ◇ ◇ ◇ ◇ ◇ ◇ ◇ ◇ ◇ ◇ ◇ ◇ ◇ ◇ ◇ ◇ ◇ ◇ ◇

**COMMON SENSE**

This 29-page pamphlet, included in chapter five of *Waking Up Together,* may be ordered separately. Your first copy is free—
see next page.
After that, the following rates apply:

        1–4 copies, $1.50 each
        5–9 copies, $1.25 each
        10–99 copies, $1.00 each
        100 or more copies, $.75 each

Use coupon or a plain sheet of paper. Total postage charge is $1.00 regardless of the size of your order. Thus, 10 *Common Sense* cost $11. (plus 60¢ sales tax if you live in California).

## ATTENTION

Whether or not you order any books, you can receive a *free* copy of Paul Williams' pamphlet *Common Sense* by sending in the coupon below or writing your name and address on a sheet of paper with the words, "Please send me a free copy of *Common Sense.*"

## COUPON

This coupon may be cut out or Xeroxed, or you may put the same information—your name, address, the books you want and amount enclosed—on a plain sheet of paper and send it to us.

Make checks payable to Entwhistle Books.

Mail to:    Entwhistle Books
            Box 611
            Glen Ellen, CA 95442

- - - - - - - - - - - - - - - - - - - - - - - - - - - - - - - - - - - - -

Please send me:

_____ copies of *Waking Up Together* . . . . . . . . $_____

_____ copies of *Das Energi* (paperback) . . . . . . _____

_____ copies of *Common Sense* . . . . . . . . . _____

_____ copies of *The International Bill of Human Rights* _____

List other titles, quantities and prices below:

_____ _____ _____

_____ _____ _____

_____ _____ _____

subtotal:    _____

California residents, add 6% tax:    _____

Postage (same charge no matter how large your order):  $\_\_\_1.00\_\_

**TOTAL enclosed:**    _____

☐ check here to receive your FREE copy of *Common Sense*

name:_____

address:_____

_____ zip:_____

send to/checks payable to: **Entwhistle Books**, Box 611, Glen Ellen, CA 95442